JOHN HAGEE

Day of Deception

Publishers Since 1798

THOMAS NELSON PUBLISHERS
Nashville • Atlanta • London • Vancouver
Printed in the United States of America

Published in Nashville, Tennessee, by Thomas Nelson, Inc., Publishers, and distributed in Canada by Word Communications, Ltd., Richmond, British Columbia.

Unless otherwise noted, Scripture quotations used in this publication are from THE NEW KING JAMES VERSION. Copyright © 1979, 1980, 1982, 1990 Thomas Nelson, Inc., Publishers.

Scripture quotations marked NIV are taken from the HOLY BIBLE, NEW INTERNATIONAL VERSION ®. Copyright © 1973, 1978, 1984 by International Bible Society. Used by permission of Zondervan Publishing House. All rights reserved.

Scripture quotations noted KJV are from The King James Version of the Holy Bible.

Library of Congress Cataloging-in-Publication Data
Hagee, John C.
    Day of deception : separating truth from falsehood in these last days / John Hagee.
        p.   cm.
    ISBN 0-7852-7573-8
    1. Christianity—United States. 2. United States—Moral conditions. I. Title.
BR526.H24   1997
277.3'0829—dc21   96-52483
                                                                CIP

Printed in the United States of America.
1 2 3 4 5 6 — 02 01 00 99 98 97

Dedication

"He who gives a book gives more than cloth, paper, ink—more than leather, parchment, and words. He reveals a foreword of his thoughts, a dedication of his friendship, a page of his presence, a chapter of himself, and an index of his love."

—Unknown

To my wife, Diana Hagee

Contents

PART ONE

Deception in Government

Chapter One

Witchcraft in the White House

He was a weak-willed, vacillating, milquetoast figure who stood for nothing but his own self-interest. His positions changed depending on who stood before him. And usually the one who stood before him was his wife who manipulated him and the government.

She was a highly motivated, politically directed feminist who knew how to use her position for personal gain. There was no doubt about it. She was the brains of the duo and as hard as nails. Her ambition was never satisfied.

Their greed was finally exposed to the nation through a mismanaged, fraudulent, real estate deal. Her fingerprints were on the incriminating government documents. At least one man died because he knew too much. But even then, she was so feared that no one dared ask too many questions.

Sound familiar? Their names were Ahab and Jezebel. They ruled as King and Queen of Israel 2,300 years ago. They wove such a web of witchcraft that the whole nation became corrupt. Government officials lied about one another. People were falsely charged and sentenced. Justice was perverted. Some were executed![1]

Only a few men of God had the courage to speak up about government persecution of the church when they were living in caves, living on bread and water smuggled to them by fellow believers. The prophet Elijah, the only one to publicly challenge Ahab and Jezebel, was so discouraged he begged God to take his life.[2]

You have probably noticed the uncanny parallel between the ancient story of Ahab and Jezebel and America's own melodrama playing out in the White House of Bill and Hillary Clinton. Like Ahab and Jezebel before them, Bill and Hillary are trying to live down their association with a fraudulent real estate deal. Fourteen people have already been convicted or pled guilty in court. Four prominent White House staffers have resigned.[3]

As this book goes to press *USA Today* reports: "The White House expects a new round of Whitewater indictments by the end of February (1997) including some present or former staffers."[4] Whitewater special prosecutor Kenneth Starr is presently taking testimony from James McDougal. White House Counsel Jane Sherburne's on-the-record acknowledgment that indictments are expected is the first by a top White House aide.

Adding to White House woes is the mysterious death of the president's attorney and Hillary Clinton's closest friend Vince Foster in Fort Marcy Park. Official police reports showed there were no fingerprints found on the gun that lay by his side. [5]

The newsrooms and pulpits of America should be in an uproar, but the newsrooms share the philosophy of today's Ahab and Jezebel and the pulpits have been frightened into submission as government agencies have finally begun the long-anticipated pulling of tax-exempt status from anyone they view as "the enemy."[6]

Talking to the Dead

Jezebel, the daughter of Ethbaal, King of the Sidonians, brought witchcraft to Israel, lending the prestige of the palace to encourage the worship of Baal. Male and female prostitutes were used in the bizarre, satanic rites that accompanied this complex but seductive form of idolatry. And in a modern age, Hillary Clinton has brought witchcraft into the White House, lending her name and influence to medium and so-called "psychic spiritualist" Jean Houston.

Hillary and Jean have met together on numerous occasions in numerous places including several meetings in the private quarters of the White House.[7] Houston claims to have a mystical link with the ancient Greek goddess Athena. The remarkable relationship between Jean and Hillary received national publicity when the news leaked that Jean Houston was leading Hillary Rodham Clinton into "imaginary conversations" with the dead, while the president of the United States sat by looking on approvingly. Allegedly, the first lady spoke with Mahatma Ghandi and her earlier predecessor in the White House, former first lady Eleanor Roosevelt, dead since 1962. According to the story, Eleanor encouraged Hillary to keep doing what she was doing. [8]

Of course, today's New Age apologists have repackaged the goods. They have taken the ancient arts and practices of divination and the occult and recast them in a whole new modern language. They talk about "white witches" who use their power for the good of mankind. They refer to mediums as "spiritual guides" and refer to necromancy as a "mental exercise." Jean Houston, the first lady's New Age "spiritual guide," has experimented with LSD, eaten magical Chinese worms, and swam with the dolphins, but today she is cloaked in respectability. [9]

The Bible is very clear. Deuteronomy 18:10–11 says, "There shall not be found among you anyone . . . who practices witchcraft, or a soothsayer, or one who interprets omens, or a sorcerer, or one who conjures spells, or a medium, or a spiritist, or one who calls up the dead."

Clinton Women

Meanwhile President Clinton continues to be plagued by a different kind of witchcraft. New details of the president's extramarital affairs keep tumbling out of the closet. The press and public are almost immune. Gennifer Flower's original story as Clinton's mistress includes hundred of pages of dates, times, and places confirmed by former Arkansas state troopers who served as Clinton security men and who have risked their careers and futures by speaking out. And yet, on the television program, *60 Minutes*, Clinton denied having an affair with Gennifer Flowers. [10]

In 1996, after being ridiculed and smeared by the press, Flowers released tape recordings of conversations she had with the president of the United States in which he called her "Darling" and "Baby" and bragged about his prowess at oral sex.[11] The media and the nation virtually ignored it.

During the 1992 presidential campaign more "Clinton women" started surfacing and journalists, egged on by Clinton political rivals, were in the hunt. A Clinton staffer, Betsey Wright, warned that there were going to be more "bimbo eruptions."[12]

Paula Jones woke up one morning after the campaign to see her own incident with Bill Clinton on the front pages. According to testimony, Jones was a young, former Arkansas state employee who had been invited up to the governor's suite. She later told a girlfriend that Clinton had closed the door, dropped his pants, and asked her to perform a sex act. Paula ran from the room, trembling and fearful. When the stories of "Clinton's women" started making another cycle in the press, a girlfriend told a journalist about Paula Jones. It was in the papers the next day.

Before Paula Jones could muster an explanation, she found herself on the front page of the nation's newspapers. One former White House aide described it as a "vicious campaign to destroy her credibility."[13] She hadn't yet said a word. By the end of the week, every private and secret deed of her life was broadcast to the world. Eventually, Paula Jones hired an attorney, hoping to stop the onslaught. The attorney promptly filed suit against the president.

Meanwhile, Bill Clinton's legal advisors have used every trick in the book to keep the Paula Jones suit from coming to court. It has been successfully stalled for years. One device has been the use of the Soldiers and Sailors Civil Relief Act of 1940. This unique law, passed on the eve of America's entry into World War II, states that civil claims against military personnel can be put off while they are on active duty. Bill Clinton, famous as a draft dodger and protester during the Vietnam War, now claimed that as president he was Commander-in-Chief and thus exempt from Paula Jones's suit.[14]

Now other information reveals that notorious San Francisco private investigator Jack Palladino was paid at least $93,000 by the Clinton-for-President campaign to help counter stories of marital indiscretion.[15] Since the Gennifer Flowers incident, Bill Clinton has been careful not to deny the many accusations that he has been unfaithful to his wife, Hillary. And yet, the pulpits of America are silent.

Exposing the Darkness

You may ask, "But doesn't the Bible also tell us to pray for those who are in authority above us? How can you be so disrespectful to our leaders?" Yes. The admonition in 1 Timothy 2:2 is very clear. As Americans we should pray for our president, for our governor, and for our representatives. We should pray for those who are in authority no matter who they are or what their political views may be. Whether they are pro-abortion or pro-life, whether they favor allowing schoolchildren the right to start their day with a silent prayer or whether they don't. But the Bible does not tell us to turn a deaf ear to evil and corruption. In 1 Peter 2:13–16, we are told how to respect those in authority over us. But in the same paragraph it instructs us to live as free men "yet not using your liberty as a cloke for vice . . ."

The Bible says in Ephesians 5:11 to expose the "works of darkness." And it warns the powerful who think they can prey on the helpless and innocent that every secret sin will be exposed.[16] The Lord, Himself, promised to be the defender of the orphan and widow. The Bible admits that for a time, evil will prosper. But Jesus warned, that whatever is whispered in secret shall be shouted from the housetop. Yes, we have a responsibility to pray for those in authority. But we have an equal responsibility to challenge corruption, defend the innocent, denounce witchcraft, and shine a light into the darkness of these latter days.

I am sometimes asked, "What right do you have to challenge government leaders?" John the Baptist boldly and publicly denounced King Herod for taking his brother's wife. It cost John the Baptist his life.[17] Jesus, Himself, had not yet met Herod when he publicly called him "that fox."[18]

Proverbs 28:4 says, "Those who forsake the law praise the wicked, but such as keep the law contend with them." There are only two positions. Either we are praising the wicked who have abandoned God's laws or we are contending with them.

King David wrote, "You who love the Lord hate evil."[19]

Jesus said, "He who is not with Me is against Me, and he who does not gather with Me scatters abroad."[20]

James writes, "Whoever therefore wants to be a friend of the world makes himself an enemy of God."[21]

God's position is very clear. You are either wheat or tares, sheep or goats, light or darkness, saved or lost.

Jeremiah was all alone in boldly denouncing the policies of King Zedekiah whom he had never met. Even the religious leaders told him, "You are a trouble maker. You are disrespectful to authority. Your words are unfair." Yet Israel was deceived, even though it was heading for destruction and the signs were there for anyone to see. Jeremiah was ridiculed and harassed. He was called the "weeping prophet" because he so despaired over the unpopular message he had to deliver. Eventually, Jeremiah was thrown into a deep pit of miry clay where he was left to die in his own human waste—but God brought him out.

Policy or Morality?

Some say to me, "Well, you're biased because you're pro-life and the president is pro-choice. This is just about abortion, an issue of policy on which honorable people disagree." They are wrong on both counts. I am not biased. I am living in a "day of deception" and hold high the torch of truth in America's darkest hour. When public policy is immoral it *should* be challenged, regardless of who is in office. In my opinion, the liberal media slander any who dare raise their voices saying they practice the "politics of hatred." It is never hatred to speak the truth. Compromise at the expense of principle is cowardice.

Dietrich Bonhoeffer stood up to Hitler in 1933, publishing a tract denouncing anti-Semitism, the de-Christianization of the school system, the new concentration camps, the legal non-accountability of the Gestapo, and the manipulation of the Reichstag elections.[22] Bonhoeffer's fellow churchmen denounced him. The Lutheran Council publicly disassociated themselves from the tract.[23] "What's wrong with Hitler?" everyone asked. "Wasn't British PM Winston Churchill saying that he 'hoped Great Britain would have a man like Hitler in time of peril?'[24] After only two years employment is restored. Our new autobahns are the wonder of the world. The new People's Car (Volkswagen) will soon make the automobile affordable to the masses. You, sir, are a trouble maker." Except for a handful of outspoken preachers, the German church was deceived.

Christians sat on their hands when the decree came down to allow abortions and "mercy killings" in hospitals. After all, the abortions were sometimes medically necessary and the mercy killings were only for mental patients who were suffering anyway. These were all "issues on which honorable people disagree." And no one raised an alarm when the word was finally given to terminate the handicapped and the invalid, including children, a great many of whom were hanged.

In 1937, when Nazi law made it illegal for churches to take collections, make proclamations, or circulate newsletters, members of Bonhoeffer's own Evangelical Confessing Church implored him to stay quiet. Later that year the government arrested 807 pastors and leading laymen in the denomination. They even blamed the preacher. "After all, he was asking for it. The Bible says to live in peace."[25]

And so these evangelical pastors sat helplessly in concentration camps when the time came for the local Jewish baker, or doctor, or neighbors, or their children's school friends to start disappearing to the so-called "resettlement camps" in the East where they were actually being murdered. And the fact is they probably wouldn't have done anything about it anyway, even if they had been free. They had been deceived.

On April 9, 1945, near the end of the war, Dietrich Bonhoeffer was taken from his colleagues at the Buchenwald concentration camp and hanged by the Nazi government he had publicly denounced for years. Two days later American soldiers liberated Buchenwald. Christians who knowingly sat on their hands while Jews went to the gas chambers were as guilty as the government leaders who made the decisions.[26]

But Elijah, the prophet, boldly stood up to Ahab and Jezebel, the powerful Bill and Hillary Clinton of ancient Israel. Ephesians 5 says, "Let no one deceive you with empty words . . . Have no fellowship with the unfruitful works of darkness, but rather expose them. For it is shameful even to speak of those things which are done by them in secret. But all things that are exposed are made manifest by the light, for whatever makes manifest is light."[27]

Nervous? It gets worse. We're only getting started. This book is not for the fainthearted! Truth is often violated by falsehood but can be equally outraged by silence.

Madison Guarantee Savings and Loan

The media are fond of confusing the public on the whole byzantine Whitewater controversy. If the public can't understand it, they certainly won't be able to make a judgment. But some aspects of the scandal are so clear, that even the media can't obfuscate. Madison Guarantee, a savings and loan of Little Rock, Arkansas, was owned by Bill and Hillary's close personal friends, James and Susan McDougal. A Senate counsel has referred to Madison Guarantee as "a thoroughly corrupt, criminal and fraudulent enterprise."[28] The McDougals and the Clintons were also co-owners of the now-infamous Whitewater land development.

Now, stay with me. Let's take one more small step. The McDougal's Madison Guarantee Savings and Loan conducted a lot of business with Capital Management Services, Inc. owned by a certain judge David Hale, at the time another friend of Bill and Hillary. Allegedly, money went back and forth between the two companies to confuse any federal regulators who might later come snooping around.

When the Whitewater development started losing money Bill and Hillary reportedly started putting the pressure on their partners, the McDougals, to take care of it. After all, he was the governor, he didn't have any money. How was he supposed to make payments on the land? One can hear Bill Clinton complain. "The whole idea was for the project to make money, lots of money. The McDougals said it would turn a profit. They should take care of it."

Today, the former judge David Hale says that then-Governor Bill Clinton pressured him into fraudulently soliciting a $300,000 government loan through Capital Services, Inc.[29] The money was then allegedly passed on to Susan McDougal, Clinton's Whitewater partner.[30] Presumably, Clinton could have boasted to the McDougal's, "Now, I did my part. You take care of the rest."

Still with me? Prosecutors now are charging two Arkansas bankers, Herby Branscum, Jr., and Robert Hill with directly funneling bank funds back into Governor Clinton's 1990 re-election campaign. The indictment is not short of detail. Among other things, it charges that on December 14, 1990, in the governor's office, one of the bankers personally handed Clinton a $7,000 contribution for the campaign he had already won. One month later, Clinton named Branscum to the State Highway Commission.[31]

Meanwhile, investigators learned that Hillary Rodham Clinton, then an attorney at the Rose Law Firm in Little Rock, Arkansas, was, in fact, the lead counsel assigned to Madison Guarantee Savings and Loan. It is not a pretty picture. If testimony is true, her husband was pushing on one end, trying to get his friend to scam the government out of some money, while on the other end his wife was providing the legal advice.

The Clintons denied everything. No, they hadn't tried to pressure David Hale or the McDougals into doing the wrong thing, and it hadn't even been proven in court that any crime had been committed in the first place. Hillary even denied she was the lead attorney for the Madison Guarantee, which would seem to be an easy thing to resolve. Either she was or she wasn't, and the billing records at the Rose Law firm would tell the tale one way or the other. And what difference did it make anyway if no one had done any of the things that were charged? When the White House was accused of covering up and pressuring witnesses to be silent they responded sarcastically, "How can you have a cover-up without a crime?" The servile press dutifully picked up the drumbeat.

Out in the Open

Then a remarkable story began filtering out of Little Rock, Arkansas. A young law clerk at the Rose Law Firm said that he and others had been given orders to start shredding documents. The special prosecutor's office immediately issued a subpoena for the billing records, making it a federal crime to destroy them. For the next two years, investigators searched through the files in the Rose Law Firm in Little Rock, Arkansas, but they searched in vain.

In a 1994 White House press conference, Hillary Rodham Clinton made it very clear, "Over the past several years, we have made a very deliberate effort to try to obtain documents, and every document that we have obtained has been turned over to special counsel, no matter where it came from."[32] It wasn't her problem.

In January 1996, it suddenly became her problem after all. A member of her own personal staff admitted under oath that she had actually seen the famous billing records on a table in the upstairs, private living quarters of the White House. She wasn't going to lie and go to jail for the first lady. Very few staffers or citizens ever see the private quarters of the White House. No one has access without the president or first lady's invitation, it is their home. At night, the president and his family are literally locked in. To no one's surprise, investigators found Hillary's fingerprints all over the documents. And to no one's surprise, they clearly showed her major role as the lead attorney for Madison Guarantee during those years of "corrupt, criminal and fraudulent enterprise." There were personal notations on the document in the handwriting of White House Counsel Vince Foster, [33] the man later found dead in Fort Marcy Park.

By the summer of 1996, the Clintons could no longer sneer about "a cover up without a crime." More than nine individuals had pleaded guilty to various crimes, spiraling out of Whitewater and its related scandals. Five others were found guilty by a jury of their peers, including judge David Hale and both James and Susan McDougal. There was now no question about whether the deed had been done. And there was no question that the crimes had benefited the Clinton's campaign and the Whitewater projects. The question was, who was lying, Bill and Hillary or everybody else?

That summer the fallout started hitting the White House as well. Bernard Nussbaum, Clinton's new counsel, resigned under pressure. He had blocked the FBI from searching Vince Foster's White House office after Foster's body was found in a public park.[34] Clinton friend, Robert Altman, Deputy Secretary Treasurer, was accused of misleading Congress, and later of improperly contacting government investigations looking into Madison Guarantee. He resigned as well, dragging two other treasury officials with him.[35] One was Treasury Chief of Staff Josh Steiner who apparently wrote some things damaging to the Clintons in his personal diary. When it was discovered, Josh stonewalled, making the incredible claim that he was lying to himself in his own diary.[36]

"Well," you say, "the president didn't get rich off of Whitewater. What's the big deal?" This is exactly the White House line. In the fall of 1993, Hillary Rodham Clinton continually complained publicly, "I'm bewildered that a losing investment . . . is still a topic of inquiry." But it is a disingenuous argument, indeed. The point is that Whitewater could have cost them a small fortune in mounting debt but government loans, fraudulently obtained, saved them. Some of the people who were sent to prison for these crimes have spoken out, openly contradicting the Clinton's version of events, but there is no one to hear them and no one who cares. To paraphrase a famous icon of the Big Apple, "only the little people go to jail."

Since the White House is always reminding the public

that Whitewater was a money-losing investment, get out your flashlight, and lets take a look at a scam that didn't lose money. The story you are about to read has never been in print. How did I get it? It walked through my door. Sometimes, when a person takes a stand, other people will get enough courage to come in and whisper their stories in secret. Now, let's shout it from the housetop.

Witchcraft on the Commodities Market

One of the more bizarre tales to come tumbling out of the Whitewater closet was how Hillary Rodham Clinton parlayed an initial investment of $1,000 into $100,000 in only one year of trading on the commodities market. The public was obviously skeptical. One critic observed sarcastically, "Put the woman in charge of investing our United States savings bonds. Maybe she can generate 1,000 percent interest for all of us? We could wipe out the national debt in three years."[37]

For a while reporters simply explained that she probably had an advisor, a seasoned, professional commodities trader, someone who made the recommendations. But then the commodities experts started weighing in on the talk shows. "No, not possible," they said. "No expert has ever been that successful with that many diverse transactions. It defies mathematical probability. Such a person would be a billionaire. They would not be a Little Rock broker." The famous Clinton research team, who answers every negative charge with a fax the next day, was uncharacteristically silent. Not one public relations genius or "spinmeister" in the country could come up with a credible explanation for the hapless Clinton White House. Couldn't be done. And yet, Hillary Rodham Clinton wouldn't even admit that she had been advised by anybody. "I relied on the *Wall Street Journal*," she said.[38]

The obvious question was, why did her magical run last only a year? If she was that good at the commodities, why didn't she keep it up? Maybe she wouldn't have repeated the phenomenal year of 1,000 percent but she might at least make a paltry 20 percent. Even that would be four times the rate of inflation. Not a bad return. Why let the money sit?

The following story came to me from the comptroller of a Fortune 500 company whose close friend ended up as a senior executive with the infamous Tyson Foods of Arkansas. The two friends met from time-to-time, each representing their own company's interests. And then, according to my source, Tyson began to "play games." The comptroller of the Fortune 500 company told his friend that, as far as he was concerned, one of Tyson's proposals amounted to outright extortion. He couldn't advise his company to go along. When he threatened to blow the whistle, he was given a hard civic lesson, Arkansas-style. "You don't understand how this state works," he was told. "We have most of the judges down here in our pocket. The young attorney general [Bill Clinton] is our man and he's going to be the next governor." When he persisted anyway, his case eventually ended up in an Arkansas court where the Tyson Company won, just as his friend had predicted. The young attorney general was now the governor.

The Fortune 500 comptroller was stunned. "Could this really be happening in the United States?" Over lunch his friend from Tyson consoled him and told the story of how they had gotten their hooks into Arkansas judges and politicians. "But the governor?" the comptroller protested. "The governor?"

"Oh, that was easy," his friend confided. "Have you ever played the commodities market? It's a pretty volatile business. You can win or lose a lot in a short amount of time. A few years ago several of us pooled our investments with a common commodities broker. He spread the money around, making a variety of investments. The young attorney general's wife threw her money into the same pot. When it was over and we had sold out, we would decide who had their money in which investment. If it was a loser, one of us would take it. If it was a winner, we would say that it had been the investment of the attorney general's wife. Then, we'd buy another round of commodities and do the whole thing all over again. Week after week. Everybody got a good laugh out of it. Of course, frequently we lost money, but even then we were winning because the attorney general's wife was getting rich, which was the whole idea."

There it is. The best explanation you'll ever get on how to turn $1,000 into $100,000 in one year. You pick your stock *after* it goes up. Can't lose.

Travelgate Tells the Story

Proverbs 14:31 says, "He who oppresses the poor reproaches his Maker." God carefully watches how the powerful treat the weak. Nothing provides a more revealing insight into a man or woman's character.

According to published reports, the Clintons had their eye on the White House travel department even before the inauguration.[39] Bill and Hillary's famous Hollywood friend Harry Thomason, part-owner of a travel consulting firm who had worked for the Clinton campaign, wrote a series of memoranda on how the White House travel department could be reorganized. He knew the travel industry and knew who should get those contracts. Soon after the election Thomason's firm had tried to muscle in on the White House travel business but had been rightly rebuffed. It was an obvious conflict of interest.[40]

Hillary was reportedly furious. The de facto president liked Thomason's ideas and, anyway, she wanted her own people running things. Why couldn't they just sweep out the current staff and bring in some loyalists? In fact,

Thomason started the process, appointing one of the president's young, Arkansas cousins to an open slot. But there was a problem.

The White House travel office was doing just fine, thank you. It was one of the most popular and smoothest running pieces in the whole White House machine. Its workers had been there for years serving presidents from both parties. But that was the problem. These were not political appointees who came and went with each administration. Billy Dale, who directed the office, had served John F. Kennedy, Lyndon Johnson, Richard Nixon, Gerald Ford, Jimmy Carter, Ronald Reagan, and George Bush.[41] These people had tenure. Legally, as government employees they could not be fired without a reason.

First the White House leaked stories charging that the travel staff was disloyal—still committed to George Bush—hoping to get some sympathetic words from their friends in the press. When that didn't work, they started accusing the office of incompetence. But that didn't resonate either. The grumpy, supersensitive, supercritical, White House press corps had nothing but praise for the White House employees. They knew them. They knew their work better than the newcomers, Bill and Hillary. Since John F. Kennedy, no other president had found them disloyal or incompetent. What was the problem?

Now, the president was really frustrated. Our modern-day Jezebel steps in. Her words were probably similar to that ancient queen's: "You're the King. Why are you sitting there so depressed? You want Naboth's vineyard? Take it! No, better yet. Stay right where you are. Let me get it for you."

According to the notes of White House Chief Mack McLarty on May 16, three days before the firings, Hillary started putting on the pressure.[42] A later memo from White House staffer Lorraine Voles says, "Hillary wants these people fired. Mac wouldn't do it."[43]

Now, why not? Weren't these people disloyal? Weren't

they incompetent? Mac McLarty, Bill and Hillary's very own chief of staff, knew that the travel office people were innocent and that it was wrong to use the White House travel office as a payoff for relatives and Arkansas friends.

When McLarty wouldn't do the dirty deed, Hillary Clinton apparently conspired with her closest friend, the president's counsel Vince Foster. According to a memorandum written by David Watkins, White House Director of Administration, "Foster regularly informed me that the first lady was concerned and desired action—the action desired was the firing of the travel office staff." Watkins, himself a friend of Bill and Hillary, was writing the memorandum to McLarty, explaining after-the-fact what had happened. "We knew that there would be hell to pay . . . we failed to take swift and decisive action in conformity with the first lady's wishes."[44]

According to FBI interviews and White House documents, "In the days before White House travel office workers were fired, Hillary Rodham Clinton pressed top presidential aides, including the chief of staff, to get the employees 'out of there.'" [45]

Watkins's own notes on a meeting with Hillary quote her as saying, "We need these people out. We need our people in."

When nothing worked, Hillary took a page from the story of Jezebel and the book of 2 Kings. Jezebel had arranged for the local authorities to falsely charge Naboth with a long list of crimes. He was brought to "justice" by his peers and with the influence and power of the palace, found guilty. In the story of Bill and Hillary, a White House lawyer, William Kennedy, called in the FBI ordering them to investigate the travel office telling them that the whole issue was being "followed at the highest levels of the White House."

Meanwhile, pressured by Hillary, David Watkins arranged for an outside auditing firm to investigate the office. A quick observation from the firm noted that the office lacked a sense of "financial control consciousness."

That was good enough for Watkins. After all, the FBI was investigating them! The seven travel office employees were summoned to his office and immediately fired. Do not pass go. Do not collect your $200. When they returned to their desks to clean out any personal materials, their replacements, including Clinton cronies from Arkansas, had already taken their places. The stunned workers were hustled outside of the building and into the back of a van. Billy Dale, the man who had served eight presidents, sat on the wheel hub. They were driven outside the gates, taken to the Ellipse in front of the Washington Memorial, and ordered to get out. Now, pay attention kids, that's how you take Naboth's vineyard!

Then the White House launched into high gear, bombarding the press with negative stories charging that the former travel office employees were guilty of embezzlement and all sorts of misdeeds. Billy Dale, who had served his country for a lifetime, was squashed like a bug.

Jezebel wanted that vineyard. Dale spent his life savings defending himself in court. The FBI, under pressure from the White House to find something, poured over ever piece of paper Billy Dale had ever written or signed. When his daughter returned home from her honeymoon, the FBI was there to ask her how she paid for it? In Psalm 12:5 the Bible declares, "For the oppression of the poor, for the sighing of the needy, / Now I will arise," says the Lord; / "I will set him in the safety for which he yearns." Clinton's justice department prosecuted Billy Dale but in the end, after spending everything he had to defend himself, he was still found innocent by a jury of his peers.[46]

When Morality Doesn't Matter

"Well," you say, "what do the Clintons say about all of this? There are two sides to everything." And the answer, is they deny it all. Hillary denies that she was the lead Rose Law Firm attorney for Madison Guarantee, even while her own billing records show the opposite. She denies she recruited them as a client, contradicting testimony from Madison Guarantee executives Gary Bunch and John Latham and her own colleagues from the Rose Law Firm, attorneys Richard Massey and Ronald Clark.

She denies that she had anything to do with the travel office firings or that she even knew there was a travel office, in spite of dozens of memos from her own staff, including notes from the replacements brought in from Arkansas.[44] She says she can't remember the David Watkins memos. The exasperated, distinguished columnist William Safire called the first lady a "congenital liar."

The president denies that he knew anything about any of the firings until it was all over, but documents obtained by the Associated Press show that he knew about the firings before they happened and that the very week of the firings he met twice with Hollywood producer and White House travel office re-organizer, Harry Thomason.[47] But mostly, the Clintons can't remember. Columnist Doug Bandow says that, "the first lady, family friends, and administration officials have responded to various investigators' inquiries with 'I don't recall' nearly 1,000 times."[48]

"Well," you say, "what difference should that make to a preacher? So, they lie. Lots of politicians lie. So, they hurt innocent people. Lots of politicians hurt innocent people. So, they steal or take a little bit for themselves. Lots of policitians steal; in fact, everybody steals. What does that have to do with preaching the gospel that Jesus saves? Quit trying to run the country. Stick to your pulpit. Leave those things to Rush Limbaugh. Do your job."

And the answer is this. Most of the Bible is written by heads-of-state or to heads-of-state. The Pentateuch, the first five books of the Bible, was written by Moses, the leader of Israel. The books of Joshua and Judges are the biographies of national leaders. Both books of Samuel, the two books of the Kings, and the two books of the Chronicles are all accounts of the public history of the Israelite nation and how God worked through the good and evil rulers of its government. The Psalms were written by King David. His son, King Solomon, wrote three more books of the Bible: Ecclesiastes, Song of Solomon, and Proverbs. The major and minor prophets wrote to the nation or to the leader of the nation, and their writings all involved public policy and its relationship to God's law. Revelation is written about the "judgment of the nations." Godly men and women cannot ignore the events of their nation. They will some day be held accountable for what they said or did not say in the face of evil. If godly men and women would stand up in the marketplaces and the pulpits of America and speak the truth fearlessly, exposing darkness, calling evil by its name, America wouldn't need Rush Limbaugh.

The Bible gives a very clear warning in 1 Corinthians 6:9–11, saying that neither the greedy, nor adulterers, nor the sexually immoral, nor swindlers will ever inherit the kingdom of God. And once more it begins its warning with those words, "Do not be deceived!"

"Well," you say, "there are crimes worse than these. Ahab and Jezebel were murderers. Maybe Bill and Hillary were greedy and insensitive to the little guy in Travelgate. Is that a crime? And maybe the president's personal life has been immoral. But then, so are a lot of other people's lives. Let's forgive and forget. Granted, that witchcraft business may be playing with fire. It could possibly get dangerous, and we probably wouldn't know it until it was too late. But you can't really believe that a modern, educated woman like Hillary Rodham Clinton could be influenced by some ancient mumbo jumbo, do you? The Madison Guarantee Savings and Loan may very well have been a criminal enterprise but that was back when he was the governor. Cut some slack."

This is America's great tragedy. She is deceived. She acknowledges evil and is not concerned. Remarkable polls made public in 1996 showed that most Americans didn't trust their president and public officials, and at the same time, most Americans didn't care that they were untrustworthy. Jeremiah the prophet saw the same thing happen just before Israel's terrible judgment at the hands of Babylon. He wrote about the nation's "casual harlotry."[49] David wrote about a time when "the wicked prowl on every side, when vileness is exalted among the sons of men." [50]

Make no mistake about it, don't be deceived; morality matters to God. John writes in the book of Revelation that God will exclude "sorcerers and sexually immoral and murderers and idolaters, and whoever loves and practices a lie" [51]

Revelation 21:6–8 establishes God's standard, "I will give of the fountain of the water of life freely to him who thirsts. He who overcomes shall inherit all things, and I will be his God and he shall be my son. But the cowardly, unbelieving, abominable, murderers, sexually immoral, sorcerers, idolaters, and all liars shall have their part in the lake which burns with fire and brimstone, which is the second death."

"Well," you say, "at least nobody got killed in Whitewater."

Read on.

Chapter Two

Who Killed Vince Foster?

They were like three peas in a pod. Webster Hubbell, Vince Foster, and Hillary Clinton. They made up the litigation department of the Rose Law Firm in Little Rock, Arkansas. Foster and Clinton had offices next to each other. Hubbell was across the hall. Other lawyers and clients often got confused. The trio was always in one another's offices or holding conferences together in the hallway.

Vince Foster and Hillary Clinton were especially close. They had lunch together almost every day. Friends say one would start a sentence and the other could finish it.[1] On special occasions, when the families of the firm got together and the men were off to the golf courses, Vince and Hillary always stayed behind to "talk." Inevitably, the gossip around town suggested that they were having an affair.[2] If nothing else, when stories of Bill's womanizing would get to Hillary, Vince was a shoulder to cry on.

When Bill Clinton became president of the United States, Webster Hubbell and Vince Foster moved to Washington, D.C., to become associate attorney general and deputy White House counsel respectively. The trio was intact.

Vince Foster was now working close-by in the west wing of the White House. When Hillary Rodham Clinton wanted something done, she could count on Foster. He handled her blind trust and other personal legal matters.[3] She went to him with her new plans for the White House travel office. It was one of his colleagues, a White House attorney, who finally ordered the FBI to investigate Billy Dale and his people. When after two years, the potentially incriminating billing records from the Rose Law Firm mysteriously surfaced in the private quarters of the White House, records further drawing Hillary into the whole Whitewater vortex, no one was surprised to see Vince Foster's handwritten notes along the margins. If anybody knew the secrets of Bill and Hillary Clinton, this man did. He was more than a lawyer who could claim confidentiality. He was a friend who could be trusted to keep a secret.

And yet, from that moment, July 20, 1993, when Vincent Foster's body was found in Fort Marcy Park, the White House of Bill and Hillary Clinton has seemed to block every legitimate attempt to solve the hundreds of attendant mysteries. Instead of leading the charge, raising a public cry to get to the bottom of what happened, calling for public support to help locate the people seen near the body, to solve the inconsistencies with the gun and the reported neck wound, they have seemingly rushed to have the whole affair buried with the body. I believe they have even used all their influence with media to hush the whole affair. Relatives and White House staffers have been told they don't have to talk to police. Curiously, it appears to me that the only person still patiently trying to put the pieces together is the independent prosecutor Kenneth Starr, the same man who was assigned by a bipartisan Congress to pursue the crimes of Whitewater.

When Cain killed Abel, the Bible says Abel's blood cried out to God from the ground demanding justice. Likewise, the facts surrounding the death of Vince Foster cry out to God demanding answers. Foster, who was the highest public official to die of mysterious circumstances since the assassination of John Kennedy, is not alive to tell us anything, but the evidence speaks with troubling clarity.

Fort Marcy Park

Ironically, the first record of any knowledge of Vincent Foster's death comes from police officers in Arkansas who, in sworn depositions, say they were informed at 6 p.m. EST. One of them immediately passed the report onto the Arkansas governor's wife. Likewise, the initial report of Chelsea's nanny claims that the White House knew of the death at 6 p.m. Everyone else there, including the president and first lady, would deny they had any knowledge until almost three hours later.[4]

The person who found Vincent Foster's body is identified in FBI reports as C.W. or "confidential witness." He was, of course, very curious. It isn't everyday that you take a walk in the park and find a corpse. He told FBI investigators that without touching the body he examined Foster very carefully. He was within eighteen inches of Foster's face. The head was laid back, looking straight up. There were no bloodstains on his face, but it was very clear he had been shot through the mouth. Both of Foster's hands were laying palms up with the thumbs pointed away from the body. There was no gun. C.W. is emphatic about that. He saw the hands. There was no gun.[5]

When the FBI later interviewed C.W. they let him know just how serious the investigation was. This was the president's lawyer. He was, perhaps, the first lady's closest friend. There would be a lot of media attention. He would have to give a sworn statement. He could get in very serious trouble if he misrepresented any fact. C.W. said he understood. He had answered every question carefully and accurately, and he would continue to do so.

C.W. testified in his sworn deposition that the vegetation under Foster's feet and on the path had obviously been trampled. He saw a half-empty wine cooler bottle near the body. As he raced back to the parking lot looking for help, the confidential witness saw a white Nissan parked in the lot. Inside was a half-full package of wine cooler bottles similar to the one beside the body. There was also a briefcase and a suit jacket that matched Foster's dress pants.

The second person to approach the scene was park police officer Kevin Fornshill. Contradicting C.W., he would later tell a reporter from the CBS show *60 Minutes* that the vegetation near the body was undisturbed. But in his repeated statements to the Senate Whitewater Committee, as well as to the FBI, Fornshill also emphatically stated: There was no gun.

Within short succession the police and paramedics began arriving. By then there was mass confusion with people coming and going. George Gonzalez, lead paramedic and the first medical person to examine the body, was suspicious. He later told the Congressional Committee on Government Operations that it is "odd to have the body laid out like it was. I wouldn't expect the hand or body in the position found, the hands perfectly at the side."[6] One paramedic listed the death as a homicide on his report.[7]

The police now found a gun in Vince Foster's right hand. There was blood on his cheek. There was no wine cooler bottle. Had the C.W. been mistaken? Had officer Fornshill been wrong? Or had someone tampered with the crime scene, placing a gun in Foster's hand?

There was no question that Foster had been shot though the mouth. But police were confronted with a conundrum. The gun was a Colt .38. It should have blown off the back of his skull. There were no skull bone fragments, brain matter, or splattered blood nearby. Nor could anyone find the bullet. And how did Foster get there? There were no car keys: not in his pocket; not in his car. Nor had anyone yet found a suicide note. But that might be at home or in his office.

Then there was a problem with the car. The white Nissan was no longer in the parking lot. But Vince Foster did not own a white Nissan. He owned a gray Honda that was found in the parking lot, parked on the other end. C.W. later told the FBI that he had not walked to that end of the lot but he was very observant, mindful that this was a crime scene. But he had seen the white Nissan. He had looked through the windows and seen the wine coolers, and the brief case, and the matching jacket. The police found none of those things in Foster's gray Honda. Nor did they find his car keys.

Fairfax County EMS technician Richard Arthur noticed a small caliber bullet hole in Foster's neck. It was on his right side, halfway between the ear and the tip of the chin. Later, George Gonzalez, lead paramedic on the scene, told investigators he also remembered a second bullet wound.[8]

Dr. Haut, the Fairfax County medical examiner, arrived at the scene some time later. By then the body had been rolled over. According to his FBI report, Haut described a "small" amount of blood behind Foster's head. The blood was matted and clotted, not liquid. Corey Ashford, one of the medical technicians who helped carry the body away, reported to the FBI that there was no blood on the ground.[9]

Dr. Haut described the exit hole in Foster's head as very small.[8] James G. Rolla, the lead investigator for the park police, was early on the scene. He, too, reported a "small" exit wound. Both testimonies would later cause confusion. An exit wound from a .38 caliber weapon would not make a "small" wound. Was another gun actually used? Haut would change his mind later and say that the wound couldn't have been small. Yet, both conclusions were first impressions of two separate professionals, each made without discussing it with the other.

The White House Reacts

Later that night, lead park investigator James G. Rolla visited Vince Foster's house to break the news to Foster's wife, Lisa. Webster Hubbell and David Watkins arrived at the same time. Rolla asked Lisa if her husband had been upset or depressed?

"No," she said, "he was very happy." And then she asked if her husband had shot himself through the mouth? Webster Hubbell told Lisa that she did not have to talk to police and everyone clammed up. Testimony was over.

President Clinton and his entourage arrived at the home soon after. If police investigator Rolla ventured a question, Clinton glared back at him.[11] The investigator finally left. He would drive to the morgue to take a more thorough look at the body. Lisa Foster would not be available to talk to police again for ten crucial days.

Park police investigators now telephoned the White House, asking to take a look in Vince Foster's office. Foster's boss, White House Counsel Bernard Nussbaum, said no. Later, when the FBI was finally brought into the case, they made a similar request. They were also turned down. Meanwhile, within the first twenty-four hours, Vince Foster's pager and all of his personal effects were returned to the White House before investigators could catalog or examine them. The computer in his office was exchanged for another. Months later an old computer with the same serial number as Foster's would show up in the White House computer repair shop. The hard drive had been destroyed.[12]

Denied access to the victim's family, his office, his computer, and official papers, including his scheduling book, park police then asked that Foster's White House office be sealed. According to the congressional record and testimony from Secret Service agents assigned to White House security, for the next twelve hours, late into the night, Clinton officials searched Vince Foster's office, taking Whitewater and other related documents out with them. Bernard Nussbaum, Patsy Thomeson, Chief of White House Personnel, and Hillary Clinton's own Chief of Staff, Mrs. Williams, conducted the search.

Then even stranger things began to happen. The car keys suddenly showed up. They were found in Foster's front pocket when the body arrived at the morgue, a pocket the police had already searched.

Even more troubling, lab reports came back showing no fingerprints on the gun. Later at FBI laboratories, the gun was taken apart piece by piece. The extensive research even revealed fingerprints made at the factory where the gun was manufactured years before, but still no fingerprints on the outside of the weapon. Had Foster put a bullet in his head and then wiped the pistol clean before taking it back into his hand?

The autopsy was performed by Dr. James Beyer, a coroner with a history of mistaking homicide for suicide. In 1989 he ruled that a Timothy Easley had stabbed himself in the chest. He didn't notice trauma to the young man's hand, a wound consistent with defensive action. An outside expert took on the case and Easley's girlfriend admitted to the murder.[13]

In 1991, in a case similar to that of Vince Foster, Beyer had ruled that a Mr. Thomas Burkett had killed himself with a gunshot wound to the mouth. The family had their doubts. The body was eventually exhumed and a second coroner discovered a broken jaw, a disfigured ear, and other evidence indicating a struggle. It obviously was not a suicide. At this writing the FBI is investigating.[14]

Nevertheless, that night, even before park investigator Rolla was able to take a close look at the body, it was officially announced that Vincent Foster had committed suicide.

The following morning the White House announced that the FBI would not be called into the case. It would be pursued by the park police. Investigator Rolla, who had never conducted a homicide investigation in his life, would have to plod on. The FBI was stunned. One agent remarked on the irony that the FBI had been called in to get rid of the travel office but weren't needed to follow through on the mysterious death of the number three man in the White House.[15]

That week, routine police work was prompting even more questions. The Saudi Arabian ambassador to the United States lived across the street from Fort Marcy Park.

His security guards were on duty very close to the actual scene of the crime, but no one heard any shots. Vince Foster's shoes were clean. There were no grass stains or dirt or pieces of vegetation even though he had walked seven hundred yards to the second cannon in the park. There were carpet fibers or blond hair on Foster's clothing. Had the body been rolled up in a carpet and carried into the park? Had Foster been killed elsewhere? We may never know. Fibers and hairs on Foster's clothing and body would never be matched with fibers or hairs from his automobile.

Then, a new witness surfaced. Patrick Knowlton had been in Fort Marcy Park just one hour before C.W. discovered the body. When he pulled into the parking lot there were only two other cars. Vince Foster's grey Honda was not one of them. Knowlton quickly noticed a man sitting in one of the cars. As Knowlton got out of the car the man gave him a menacing stare and then opened his own car door. Knowlton walked in the opposite direction, away from the man and away from the path that led to the future scene of the crime only minutes away. The man stared after Knowlton and then got back into his car. A statement prepared by the witness and his attorney says the strange man's actions were consistent with a lookout, "as if his purpose was to prevent any passers-by from venturing into the area of the park where Vincent Foster's corpse was found one hour later."[16]

A Deepening Mystery

Great curiosity now attended the fact that there was no suicide note. But just as the keys would suddenly and conveniently appear to reassure skeptics, so the note showed up six days after the death. While the note did not suggest suicide it did talk about the anguish that Foster was experiencing in his work relating to Travelgate and Whitewater. Even though the note was not conclusive one way or the other, the way it surfaced did not reassure doubters. How had a note in his briefcase been missed in the first place? Why was it showing up now, days later? No one was surprised when it was learned that there were no fingerprints on the note. There was however a palm print. It was never matched with Foster's.

In July 1995, White House lawyer Miriam Nemetz wrote a memo quoting White House Chief of Staff Mack McLarty as saying that Hillary Rodham Clinton had favored delay in making the note public. "McLarty said that the first lady was very upset and believed the matter required further thought and that the president should not yet be told. They should have a coherent position and should have decided what to do before they told the president."[17]

In October 1995, three handwriting experts ruled that the so-called suicide note found six days after Foster's death was a forgery. Sponsored by Strategic Investment, Reginald Alton, a fellow emeritus of St. Edmund Hall, Oxford; Vincent Scalice, a former New York City police detective; and Ronald Rice, a professional handwriting analyst with eighteen years of forensic experience, all came to the same conclusion. Twelve samples of Foster's handwriting were compared to the note found in his briefcase. Each concurred that Foster couldn't have written the note. Foster, for example wrote the letter *b* with a single stroke. His forger used three separate strokes.

But such information would come later, and while each instance would raise more questions or doubts, no one single discovery would be sufficient to arouse the media or the public from its lethargy. If something sinister had happened, no one wanted to know.

Lisa Foster, the dead man's wife, was finally interviewed ten days later her husband's death. She was shown a silver gun and asked if it belonged to her husband. She admitted that it looked like the silver revolver she had sometimes seen around the house. Yet later, when ABC television obtained one of the photographs of the death scene, it clearly showed that the gun in Foster's hand was black, not silver. This was confirmed by the first Senate investigation, which also revealed that the gun was assembled from two different Colt revolvers with two separate serial numbers stamped on their pieces.[18]

The controversy over the gun would continue to fester. Neither the FBI nor the police could confirm that the silver gun shown to Lisa Foster did, in fact, belong to her husband. Only two bullets were found in the weapon and, remember, the first two persons to find the body said there was no gun at all. No matching bullets were ever found in the Foster home, automobiles, or at the crime scene. Nor was any proof forthcoming that the gun found with the victim fired the fatal shot.[19]

There would also be little chance for leaks of photos or any other evidence. First, most of the Polaroid photos of the crime scene vanished. Then it was learned that all 35mm film of the crime scene was "overexposed" or disappeared and Dr. Beyer's X-rays were "misplaced" and never recovered. Meanwhile, all police and paramedics at the scene were ordered not to discuss the case.[20]

Independent prosecutor Robert Fiske eventually completed a report determining that Vince Foster had indeed committed suicide, but the report was so riddled with inaccuracies, it only contributed to the controversy. Dr. Haut was now changing his testimony to fit the new scenario. Leads were not followed. Questions were left up in the air. Robert Fiske's hard-driving staffer, an assistant U.S. attorney, Miguel Rodriquez, resigned in disgust, not wanting to be part of a cover-up.

Part of the criticism was directed toward the weak motive for the alleged suicide. Foster had eaten a full lunch, joked with his staff, and promised to be right back when he drove off to his rendezvous in Fort Marcy Park. Foster's friend and attorney, Jim Lyons, was coming from Colorado to meet with him the next day and Foster had expressed eagerness to show him around. Likewise, he had double checked to make sure he would be free to take his sister on a personal White House tour the next morning. His appointment book, critical to the running of his office and, incidentally, critical to the investigation, was never found. As in the case of the police pictures and the X-rays taken at the autopsy, it disappeared into the firmament.

Eventually, Congress enlisted Kenneth Starr as a more forceful independent prosecutor. Robert Fiske was gone. Starr was viewed as less likely to be influenced by his partisan Democrat superior, Mark Tuohey IV. Likewise, two journalists picked up the trail of the Foster death giving some public exposure to controversial facts that the rest of the media were ignoring.

The Media to the Rescue

Once more, the CBS television production, *60 Minutes*, came to the rescue of Bill and Hillary Clinton. During the campaign of 1992, when the stories of Clinton's promiscuity had reached its most critical stage, *60 Minutes* gave the Clintons a national audience. Mr. Hewlett, producer of the show had been quoted as saying he could have buried Bill Clinton's presidential chances in the snows of New Hampshire if he had been so inclined.[21] He was not. And this time his program sought to answer the growing questions regarding the Vince Foster affair.

60 Minutes ignored the paramedics and their reports. None of them were interviewed. The show even ignored the confidential witness, telling their national audience that a park policeman was the first person to discover the body. It was absolutely false. A bold misrepresentation. But then, who reads or pays attention? When they did interview someone, the testimony was very selective. Park policeman Kevin Fornshill was given a chance to say that the ground around the body was not trampled, lending credence to the theory that there was no struggle at the scene of the crime but Fornshill was not asked about his report that there had been no gun in the victim's hand.

Later, the FBI revisited C.W., the "confidential witness" who had first found the body. He had told them that the vegetation under Foster's feet and on the path nearby was trampled. This was now a public issue. Was he sure about his facts? C.W. insisted that he was. He offered some helpful speculation. If it were a suicide, the dead man may have been pacing before he shot himself. But it was definitely trampled. And it would have taken a lot to flatten the vegetation. C.W. was actually taken to the crime scene twice by the FBI, each time answering the same way.

60 Minutes ignored altogether any critical questions about the gun, or the lack of fingerprints, or the so-called suicide note, focusing most of their attention on the differing testimony about the blood at the scene. Dr. Haut's testimony to the FBI was never mentioned, while the new version of his testimony was featured. Viewers were not told of the discrepancy.

The *coup de grace* was a clever strawman built out of the fact that critics were suggesting Foster was left-handed when the gun was found in his right hand. *60 Minutes* triumphantly informed the nation that this was all bogus. Foster was indeed right-handed. But this was not an issue of serious critics who already knew Foster was right-handed. The point was that the first official and non-official persons to arrive at the scene were insistent that there was no gun at all, not in either hand. Such testimony was ignored.

The program had its intended impact. Much of the public furor driving the independent prosecutor's investigation into Foster's death was deflated. But the most powerful revelation concerning Vince Foster was yet to come.

Two journalists, Chris Ruddy of the *Pittsburg Tribune-Review* and Ambrose Evans-Pritchard of the *London Sunday Telegraph,* had been snooping around the fat edges of the Foster scandal for months. Evans-Pritchard was able to determine that Vince Foster had made at least two secret, unofficial trips to Switzerland. He had canceled a third visit only twelve days before his death. His own wife, Lisa Foster, had no knowledge of the trips. This was remarkable, almost unbelievable news. But the story was soon confirmed and published in the Telegraph. What was Foster doing in Switzerland?[22] Still, for the most part, a strangely silent media looked on with disinterest.

Meanwhile, key witnesses, whose testimony raised doubts about the favored suicide theory, found themselves the target of harassment. These people had only done their duty as citizens. In no case had any of them written books or demanded money from tabloids or commercialized their information in any manner. C.W. was still anonymous. The others usually refused any requests for interviews. None were deemed partisan or critics of the administration.

Patrick Knowland, the man who had witnessed suspicious people in the park just before the body was found, was followed around the streets of Washington, D.C. Sometimes his antagonists would openly harass him or glare at him. Knowland contacted a lawyer who made a careful record of each instance, which constituted clear violations of federal law prohibiting "tampering with a witness, obstruction of justice, or any intimidation of a witness." The lawyer wrote that the number of persons used in the surveillance of Mr. Knowland and their expert knowledge of his daily routine suggested enormous resources at work.

Suicide or Murder?

What happened in Fort Marcy Park that summer of 1993? Was Vincent Foster murdered? Was he advocating a course of action that would have been embarrassing to powerful people? Or did he really commit suicide? Do all of the incriminating circumstances relate only to the crimes of Whitewater or are there other embarrassments that powerful people feared might have come tumbling out of the closet if the police had looked too closely? Either explanation, of course, points to a crime.

And what has happened to the country whose sensibilities were once aroused over Watergate and the "bugging" of the offices of one political party by activists working to promote the cause of the other? You will remember that President Richard Nixon was driven from office, not because he authorized or even knew about the action, but because he covered up a crime committed by others.

Today, we openly talk about the cover-up of Whitewater. No one seems to care. Not the press, not the church, not the public. To criticize the sexual infidelities of public officials is viewed as judgmental and intolerant. And the number three man at the White House just may have been murdered. Webster Hubbell, the former deputy attorney general of the United States and a close friend of both Hillary Clinton and Vincent Foster says, "One thing for sure, Vince Foster did not kill himself."[23] But we are all into self-denial. A series of coincidences and accidents, we tell ourselves. We don't want to face the responsibility of knowing the details or the facts, so we hide behind the comforting thought that it is just too incredible to be true. We know that teenagers are murdered for their designer tennis shoes on the streets outside our door but surely not Vince Foster. We are deceived.

David speaks of a time when, "The wicked in his pride persecutes the poor . . . In the secret places he murders the innocent . . . . Arise, O Lord! O God, lift up Your hand! Do not forget the humble."[24]

At the Rose Law Firm in Little Rock, Arkansas, they were three peas in a pod. Webster Hubbell, Vincent Foster, and Hillary Rodham Clinton. Today, Webster Hubbell is peeling potatoes in a federal penitentiary, Vince Foster is dead, and Hillary Clinton is ruling her kingdom from the White House. But all three will one day bow before the

Lord, who is judge above all. And each will answer for every word and deed. Until that day, do not be deceived; God is not asleep. He is watching and listening. Though "what is vile is honored among men" and the "wicked freely strut about," He will rise to action in these latter days. He always has. He always will. God is faithful to keep His Word!

Chapter Three

Who Controls America?

In the early 1990s President George Bush and Secretary of State James Baker seemed to be in a political footrace to see who could use the latest and most trendy political phrase "New World Order." President Clinton, sensitive to the criticism of millions of Americans, has cleverly avoided the expression, but the policies they represent remain on the fast track with no interruption or challenge in sight.

The concept of a "New World Order" is nothing new. It was the driving principle on the plains of Shynar where Nimrod proposed to build the tower of Babel almost four thousand years ago. The purpose of the tower of Babel was to defy the authority of God and to drive Him out of the affairs of men. It was satanic and demonic, manifesting itself by the occult symbols that were attached to its side.

In twelfth century B.C., the Babylonian kingdom became the first of several great empires to rule the civilized world. From a purely historical standpoint, the Babylonian era was the most glorious and most evil of any that followed. The Jews, God's chosen people, were once more dragged off into slavery.

The Medes and the Persians were the next great empire to achieve world domination. Their kingdom, steeped in idolatry, stretched from middle Europe to India.

According to revisionist historians the most progressive one world order was established by the Greeks. Today's schoolchildren are taught that the glorious Greece of antiquity practiced the purest form of democracy; but, in fact, their experiment with freedom was brief and limited. More than half of the population of ancient Greece were slaves. And of those who were "free," half were women who could not vote, own property or testify in court; they were not even counted in the official census. The famous pure Greek democracy, praised by modern educators, was fine if you were one of the lucky 25 percent.

For years the government and social life of the Greek empire and its one-world order was dictated by the Pythia, the mysterious Oracle of Delphi. Priests would take an ordinary peasant woman, invoke "the spirits," and when she finally fell into a trance they would submit their list of questions to her. Through the peasant woman, the Pythia for the day, the spirits would miraculously speak back, sometimes in various languages.[1]

The Roman empire, the last successful "world order," was virulently anti-Semitic and anti-Christian. In 70 A.D., the Romans, under General Titus, finally destroyed Jerusalem. Under the emperor Nero, Christians were fed to the lions in Rome and hung as grotesque human torches for his garden parties.

In the great temptation of Jesus, Satan, himself, proposed a "New World Order." "All these things I will give you," he says, "if You will fall down and worship me." And understand, they were Satan's to give.[2] Today, he is still offering that promise. Through a seemingly benign and benevolent world statesmen, he is promising a world without war and an end to hunger—heaven on earth. But the Bible says it will soon turn into a living hell.

The Illuminati

In more recent centuries there has been the confusing and mysterious story of the Illuminati. There have been so many exaggerated and unfounded theories written about this organization and its history that it can be a chore to separate fact from fiction. What we know is this: The Illuminati did exist. It was a super-secret, European organization of international financial power brokers whose initial goal was to bring about worldwide economic stability but whose quick success, and sometimes very hostile resistance, prompted the more grandiose goal of worldwide dominion. Born at a time of great rebellion against the corrupt, organized church and influenced by the radicalism of the French Revolution, their leadership was exclusively atheistic with the notable exception of several committed, practicing satanists.[3]

At various times in recent centuries, the power and reach of this organization within world financial and governmental circles has been astounding—a virtual banking-governmental mafia. Look on the backside of an American dollar bill and you will see the three Latin words, *Novus Ordo Seclorum,* "One World Order." These words are carried on a waving banner just under a pyramid and topped by an all-seeing eye. Some say this all-seeing eye represents providence. Others say it represents the eye of the ancient Egyptian deity, Osyrus. This remarkable seal approved by Congress in 1782 was designed by Charles Thompson, a member of the Masonic order who served as the secretary of the Continental Congress.[4]

Hitler's Attempt

In his 1932 election bid, Adolf Hitler told the people of Germany, "If you will elect me as the Fuhrer of this nation, I will introduce a New World Order that will last a thousand years." A compilation of Hitler's speeches, published in English, was appropriately entitled My New Order.

Only in the decade after the Nuremberg Trials did researchers begin to understand how deep-seated and mystical was the pagan and satanic ritual embraced by many of the Nazi leaders. Heinrich Himmler, leader of Hitler's infamous SS and the man entrusted with the diabolical orders to exterminate the Jews, embraced a wide range of pagan and satanic beliefs that would be considered "New Age" by the naïve of today. For Himmler and his SS, Christian rites of christening, marriage, and death were replaced by neo-pagan ones. The Christmas holiday became Julfest and was changed to December 21. Initiation rites for highest SS officer recruits included taking an oath before sixteen blazing altars towering three stories tall, the obelisks of the *Feldherrnhalle*, the Nazi Temple of Honor in Munich. The names of sixteen martyred Nazis were intoned by a voice-over and the new officers would shout, "Present." Himmler himself believed in reincarnation, telling people that he was really a new manifestation of King Heinrich of the Saxons. In 1937 he had the bones of the ancient king interred at Quedlinburg Cathedral.[5]

The eminent historian Francis Miller suggests that twenty million people died because of Hitler's "new order," including six million innocent Jewish men, women, and children.[6]

The Communist Deception

Even before Hitler and his gang were buried, Stalin and a small criminal society controlling the Soviet Union began secretly planning their own New World Order. Stalin's eventual successor, Nikita Khruschev, once announced to Richard Nixon, "We will bury you."

By the mid-1960s the sheer volume of Soviet horrors was hard to deny. Eye witnesses spoke of millions of innocent people consigned to virtual slave labor in Siberia and others spoke of millions dying in the prison camps in the Gulags. In 1963, in an audacious attempt to regain international credibility, Khruschev blew the lid on many of those state secrets, admitting that Stalin was a criminal who had consigned millions of innocent people to their deaths but that the Soviet Union had now abandoned its insane ideas of conquering the world and was seeking to make the ideal of communism and humanism really work.[7]

Communism was a powerful and intellectually seductive concept, so brilliant and sincere, people were drawn into its vortex. But behind its benevolent, humanitarian promises was a violent and hideous reality. Both Jews and Christians were murdered and persecuted for their beliefs. During the malevolent reign of Pol Pot's Khmer Rouge in Cambodia, the nation was turned into a "killing fields." Pol Pot marked for execution all doctors, nurses, teachers, and government workers. All members of the media, clergy, anyone associated with the arts, the theater, and ballet were also marked for execution. If you wore eye glasses you were put on the list, because if you wore eye glasses you could probably read, and if you could read they would have to kill you. Incredibly, Pol Pot is still alive. Though he and his armies have been driven into the jungles, no one is calling him to accountability—not the United Nations, not the United States, no one. No one is calling for a modern Nuremberg Trial for this ruthless Oriental Hitler of our generation.

In the late 1980s, Mikhail Gorbachev tried to do again what Nikita Khruschev had done twenty years before. Once more the lid was blown off communism and a new Soviet leader admitted to the crimes of his predecessors, including not only Leonid Brezhnev, but the phony reformer Nikita Khruschev, himself. But this time it didn't work, and the Soviet empire collapsed like a house of cards.

The United Nations

After World War I, President Woodrow Wilson became the most famous public voice calling for a one world order.

The League of Nations failed, but the idea surfaced again after Hitler. In 1946, the United Nations was born.

On January 29, 1991, then-President George Bush announced America's launching of the war in the Persian Gulf. "What is at stake in this war is more than one small country" he said, referring to Kuwait. "It is a big idea. The idea of a New World Order."[8]

To the surprise of the Bush administration, most evangelical Christians recoiled at those words. Some associated them with secret societies (almost always anti-Semitic and anti-Christian), with Hitler's famous public boasts, or with the communist promises that turned to nightmares unless you were on the right side of the gun barrel. But most Christians associated the words with the coming holocaust prophesied in Scriptures. The great promise of a peaceful one world government that will, instead, turn this planet into a living hell.

Today, with the encouragement of the Clinton administration, the United Nations is saying we will produce this New World Order. What does it mean? When you hear it, what does it say to you? Read the words of Brock Chisham, the director of the United Nations World Health Organization. "To achieve this world government, it is necessary to remove from men their individualism, their loyalty to their families, national patriotism, and religion." [9]

During the last twenty-five years the United Nations has been transformed into a propaganda platform for the enemies of the United States and Israel. Time after time in that world body, America and Israel have stood all alone against every other member nation in the world. And sometimes we have simply been voting for Israel's right to exist. The most obscene example of the United Nations' morality took place on October 1, 1975, when the dictator of Uganda, Idi Amin, who was then chairman of the Organization for African Unity, addressed the General Assembly.

This bloodthirsty tyrant denounced an imaginary Zionist-U.S. conspiracy and called not only for the expulsion of

Israel from the United Nations but for the country's extinction.

The combined assembly gave him a standing ovation when he arrived, applauded him throughout his address, and rose again when he left. The following day the secretary-general and the president of the General Assembly hosted a public dinner in Amin's honor.[10]

"Well," you say, "from an economic and peace-keeping perspective the United Nations has been an international joke, a fiasco, an international nothing. How can powerful people now talk seriously about this organization running things? It isn't logical. It will never happen." You're wrong! This isn't about logic. It isn't about peace. It isn't about feeding hungry people. This is about power . . . worldwide power. It's about a one-world government; it's about a one-world economy; it's about absolute dictatorial control over every American citizen and the citizens of any democracy on earth.

For the Christian, the biblical account and man's own recorded history clearly show the same syndrome. The need for world domination, whether out of benevolence or greed, has ultimately been corrupted. It is almost always idolatrous, satanic, or atheistic. It is usually anti-Semitic and anti-Christian. Look at the record. Look at Babylon. Look at ancient Greece. Look at Rome, at Hitler, at Stalin and his successors. It is a demon spirit anointed in the bowels of hell to rob, to kill, and to utterly destroy.

Randall Baer, whose bestselling Harper and Row books once made him the world's New Age authority on crystals, tells about how "the cosmic gods were paving the way for me to do important work in bringing about a revolutionary *New Age, One World Order.*"[11]

Curiously, Baer, who claimed that "spirit guides" dictated his books, frequently invoked that ancient symbol associated with the Illuminati and boldly planted on the American dollar. "The spirit guides told me to take twelve quartz crystals and lay them out in a circle, to tape another one to the occult 'third eye,' and to suspend a large pyramid overhead."[12]

Jean Houston, the first lady's famous self-described "spiritual psychic" whose visits to the White House have included several lengthy stays, calls herself "a global midwife." Houston says that she works "with heads-of-state all over the world."[13] But if she is a "global midwife," just what do the New Agers want to be born?

The Antichrist

There is going to be a New World Order in these latter days. From ages past, the prophets have said it would happen. Jesus spoke of it in great detail. It will be led by Satan's messiah whom the Bible calls the Antichrist. When the world rejects truth, all that's left is a lie. When the world rejects light, all that's left is darkness. When the world rejects Jesus Christ, all that's left is Satan's messiah, the Antichrist. And God the Father is saying from the plains of Shynar and the tower of Babel to the United Nations, "Men have been trying to get rid of me, they have been trying to get rid of my Son Jesus Christ, and they have been trying to escape the Word of God. All right, I'm going to let you have a New World Order. I'm going to turn Satan's messiah, the Antichrist, loose to rule the earth with an iron fist, producing the New World Order."

He's going to turn the streets of the world into a bloodbath. According to the prophets, one-third of all humanity is going to be massacred under this monster who is going to make Adolf Hitler look like a choir boy.

The apostle John described it two thousand years ago, long before bank wire transfers or even banks. Long before there was a social security system, requiring you to have a number. Long before computer technology made such feats possible, John described how the Antichrist will control world commerce. Every person alive will receive a mark in the back of his right hand and between his eyes. Without it, you won't be able to buy or sell a shoelace. He will set himself up as the all-powerful currency controller as he institutes a one-world government and a one-world currency. Jesus warned that eventually, he will try to set himself up as God.

Revelation 13:16–17 says, "And he causes all, both small and great, rich and poor, free and slave, to receive a mark in the right hand and on their foreheads and that no man may buy or sell except one who has the mark or the name of the beast, or the number of his name."

This will be the long anticipated New World Order. But according to the prophets, Brock Chisham of the World Health Organization is at least partially correct. Four things will have to happen first.

The Destruction of Money

First, there must be the destruction of the monetary system, your currency. I believe America's economic problems were not created by market conditions but were planned and orchestrated to devalue and destroy the American dollar. This was done by that unseen government Dwight D. Eisenhower called "The Eastern Establishment."[14]

Consider the following. Our government deliberately went off the gold standard to which it was attached and on which it was founded. From the day that the dollar was removed from the gold standard it has floundered. If anyone tells you, "You look as sound as the dollar," start looking for a casket. You're in big trouble.

The major banks of America poured billions of dollars into communist governments and into third-world nations, knowing full-well that those governments had no ability or willingness to pay the money back. Why would they do that? Go to your banker tomorrow and say, "I don't have the ability to pay you back, and I don't even want to pay you back. I'd like to borrow $10 billion, please." See what the response would be.

Yet our banks, backed by our own government, gave away hundreds of billions of dollars. Why? Because what few Americans know is that the Monetary Control Act of 1980 gives the Federal Reserve Board the power to exchange U.S. dollars for third-world debt. That simply means that the banks in New York and the major banks of America controlled by the Eastern Establishment will not lose a dime but that you, America's taxpayers, are going to pay the bill.

According to Stanford University, the final bill on the failed savings and loan crisis will cost the taxpayers of America $1.3 trillion.[15] Now get a picture of this in your mind. If you start making a stack of crisp, new $1,000 bills your stack will go four inches high to equal $1 million. So how high will the stack have to get to equal $1 trillion? Remember, we are talking about $1,000 bills. The answer? A stack sixty-seven miles high will equal $1 trillion. The Savings and Loan fiasco all by itself, will cost even more.

Bankruptcies in America are at an all-time high. Mergers and hostile takeovers are putting more and more wealth into the hands of fewer and fewer people, which is exactly the cause of the crash of 1929. New bank failures are mounting. Twelve hundred and fifty-six banks are now on the Federal Regulator's problem list. If the banks follow the pattern of the savings and loans, the FDIC is going to be wiped out. Currently, there are about 1.5 pennies backing up every dollar that you have in savings.[16]

Some people have built their life around the dollar, but God is saying, "You had better build your life around Me because I'm the only thing that's going to endure." The currencies of this world are not going to endure. The kingdoms of this world are going to collapse. The only kingdom that is going to endure is the kingdom of the Lord Jesus Christ, and of His kingdom, thank God, there shall be no end.

Logical people would say, "Why can't the Congress of the United States stop the death of the dollar?" Congress does not control America's economic destiny. Our economic destiny is controlled by the Federal Reserve System. This system sets the rate of interest on the money in your pocket. When they determine this rate of interest, they determine the value of your dollars.

The Federal Reserve has no elected officials. Not one United States senator or representative sits on its board. Neither does the president of the United States or the vice president. The Federal Reserve has never been audited and yet it totally controls the value of money in this country. It was formally authorized on December 23, 1913, over a Christmas holiday, when most of the U.S. Congress was gone. It is controlled by Class A stockholders. The major stockholder in America is David Rockefeller. While most of the stockholders are members of the so-called Eastern Establishment, allegedly, the four largest stockholders are not even Americans but members of the Rothchild's family of Europe.[16]

Thomas Jefferson once said, "A private central bank issuing public currency is of greater menace to the liberties of America than an invading army."[17]

Am I worried about that? If my faith was centered around the American dollar and if all my hopes were pegged to the United States government, I'd give birth to peptic ulcers before I finished writing this book. But I am not worried because my hope is in the Lord Jesus Christ and in the authority of the Word of God. God is in charge and God is in control.

Have you ever heard of the golden rule? "Those who have the gold make the rules." God says in the book of Haggai, "The silver is Mine, and the gold is Mine."[19] He's not controlled by the Eastern Establishment, He's not controlled by the Rothchilds, He's not controlled by the Federal Reserve. He is sovereign God. He says in the book of James "Come now, rich men, weep and howl for your misery has come upon you. You have heaped gold and silver for the last days and it shall eat your flesh like fire."

People ask, "Why would God allow a financial collapse in America?" I'll tell you why. Because the First Commandment says, "Thou shall have no other gods before me." And in America, money is a god. Money has replaced our love for each other. Money has replaced our love of the family. Money has enthroned itself as lord of all. We are the generation of "instantaneous gratification." We want what we want and we want it NOW! It makes no difference what it takes to get it.

America's materialism, greed, and demand for instantaneous gratification has produced a nation of drug addicts, a nation of alcoholics, a nation that's addicted to pornography and a condom culture for "safe sex." It has taken fathers away from their children. It has destroyed marriages. We have squandered our health in the pursuit of money. We have built cathedrals of worship to the gods of money. They're called banks. When you go there tomorrow and talk to your banker be sure and hold your hat in your hand and tuck your head in reverence or you won't get what you want.

God is saying to America, "You shall have no other gods before me." The gods of America are falling. The banks are falling. The savings and loans are falling. Wall Street will eventually utterly collapse. I've got good news for you. God is not falling. He is on the throne and He is all-powerful. "For Thine is the kingdom, and the power, and the glory forever and ever."

The second thing that has to happen before the New World Order can take place is the destruction of nationalism and patriotism.

The Death of Patriotism

The unseen government—those who are pushing the

one-world government, and the New World Order, those professional politicians whose only objective is to get re-elected—are searching for ways to destroy patriotism in America, and they have been long at it.

The Korean War was a United Nations war; it was called a police action. For the first time in America's history we went to war without the objective of winning. It wasn't even in the equation. General Douglas MacArthur resigned in disgust. The old soldier from the long gray line stood before the Congress of the United States and said, "There is no substitute for victory."

History has proven General Douglas MacArthur right and the Congress of the United States wrong. There is no substitute for victory, and any time we commit American lives to the battlefield it ought to be for the purpose of victory and victory alone. It should not be as an instrument of the United Nations and its objectives or the pawn of the military-industrial complex who grow rich in a time of war.

Vietnam was a controlled war. We could not attack the enemy sanctuaries. We could not mine the harbors. As a result, America was portrayed to the world as a loser. For twelve years our sons bled and died, and we couldn't whip a nation the size of Vermont that employed medieval military techniques. Patriotism in America reached an all-time low. U.S. soldiers came home and were literally spit on by the American public. America's leaders owe the Vietnam veterans a public apology for sending them into a war where victory over the enemy was not our objective.

Why all the flag waving over the War in the Persian Gulf? To sell the American people on the idea that the United Nations is a better way of government for the community of nations. To sell the idea that the New World Order is indeed the best way to bring balance and justice to a world in chaos.

Understand that 85 percent of the membership of the United Nations consists of third-world representatives who hate America. Around the world we are called "The great

Satan." It is an economic fact that you, the taxpayers of America, pay 90 percent of the annual budget of the United Nations. The rest of the world pays 10 percent.[20]

Here's what the New World Order will mean to you nationally and spiritually as Americans and as Christians and Jews. The United Nations traditionally votes against Israel. Zionism has already been labeled by the United Nations as racism. Are you willing to send United States troops to fight Israel? That's what could very well happen if the United Nations through New World Order comes to power.

Are you willing to see the United Nations vote to redistribute the wealth of America to third-world nations? That legislation is already in place. Welcome to the New World Order. If we submit our national will to the will of a clique of international power brokers using the United Nations they could simply vote the wealth of this nation away to any other nation they desired while our Congress sat by and watched.

Are you willing for United Nations troops to appear on the streets of America and shut down every synagogue and every Bible-believing church in the country? "Preposterous," you say. And yet most delegates to the United Nations come from third-world countries, most of which are Islamic. In 1981, the General Assembly of the United Nations adopted what was called "The Declaration of the Elimination of All Forms of Intolerance and Discrimination Based on Religious Beliefs."[21] Sounds good, but it was only a new device for propagating anti-Semitism. According to fundamentalist Islamic teaching a Christian or a Jewish person has one alternative. He or she can convert to Islam or have their head cut off. It's in their bible. Welcome to the New World Order. It would also terminate Christian evangelism because evangelicals are intolerant of pagan religions and their doctrines. Unity, at the expense of truth, is the gospel of the New World Order.

The third thing that has to happen before the New World Order can assume power is the destruction of the evangelical faith.

An Attack on the Church

Now there is debate within the evangelical church over just when and how this will take place, but there is little debate about the fact that the prophets warned that a great persecution of believers would come.

Why? Because as long as you believe in the Word of God, you are loyal to the kingdom of God. You represent a government within a government and you are a hindrance to the New World Order. Your credibility and your confidence must be shaken. Your confidence must be shaken in your leaders, it must be shaken in your cause, and finally it must be shaken in yourselves. Evangelicals can expect to be attacked through the law, through the media, through Hollywood, and through the educational system under the control of the National Education Association (NEA).

Only a few years ago, when the American Bar Association, the foremost legal fraternity of America, met in San Francisco, their plenary session was "How to attack the church through tort law."

In California, a young lady answered an altar call and came down the aisle to receive Jesus Christ. Her relatives later said that the preacher used an emotional appeal to bring her to the altar, and she was psychologically damaged by being brainwashed into receiving Jesus Christ. Her parents sued the church for damages and they won.[22]

This is where many in the legal fraternity now have their mind set. Churches are seen as a source of money and are being sued for doing what they were organized to do, preach the gospel of Jesus Christ. Parishioners and pastors are having to spend their time and money to defend their right to worship according to their beliefs. This is not something that is coming to America. It's here!

In 1990, the U.S. Congress passed into law the Hate Crime Bill. Police agencies are not being directed to track crimes of hate. It sounds wonderful. A blow against intolerance. But the devil is in the details. Tacked onto the end of one clause was the remarkable phrase forbidding speech "in any negative manner about a person's sexual preference."[23]

According to some interpretations, a pastor standing in his own church reading aloud the Bible verses describing homosexuality as an abomination to God is now breaking federal law. He could be fined or put in prison. This is not something that is coming. It is here—in America in these latter days.

Likewise, attacks against the church in the national media are well under way. Sadly some major ministries in America have given the media plenty to attack. When the media exposes an evangelist who sleeps with prostitutes or defrauds his own followers of millions of dollars, they are not only doing a favor to society, they are doing a favor to the church, as well. But don't be deceived by media smear campaigns. Remember much of the Bible was written from prison. But you say, "They wouldn't be in trouble if they were really innocent." Remember, Jesus was crucified by an angry mob who saw him as a blasphemer, and He was innocent. Rome saw Him as an insurrectionist too dangerous to live. The apostle Paul was innocent, yet he went to jail. The founding fathers of the church were innocent, yet martyred.

In one national case the minister's attorneys went to court and obtained from the national television network the actual raw video footage taken during their coverage of the ministry. After videotaping an interview, one of the most popular television reporters in America got in her car to leave, but unbeknownst to her and the camera crew, the videotape was still going. The video itself only showed the dashboard and floorboard of the automobile, but the audio records a remarkable conversation. America's sweetheart reporter curses and allegedly announces, "Well, he's innocent but we can destroy him anyway."

Christian bashing is now an art form in America. According to the Gallup organization more than 42 percent of the American public claim to be born-again Christians but you seldom read a positive story about them.[24] They are now blasted by the media as right wing, fundamentalist, homophobic hate-mongers! Jesus said, "You will be hated by all for My name's sake . . ."[25]

What is the driving force behind the attack? Why don't they attack all churches? Why just the Bible-preaching churches? Is it the New World Order that sees you as the government within the government? Again, the Eastern Establishment controls the major New York banks who have taken their huge multibillion dollar trust resources and bought the stocks of ABC, NBC, CBS, *Time*, and *Newsweek*. You will never read a bad word about David Rockefeller. You will never read a good word about evangelicals because we are seen as "dangerous and intolerant" by the national media.

One remarkable survey found that less than 30 percent of American journalists believed in a personal God, while 95 percent of the American public said they did believe in a personal God. Not even 3 percent of American journalists said that they attend a church or synagogue.[26] *Time* magazine, whose masthead carries the names of its 120 editors, reporters, and staff can name only two born-again journalists. *Newsweek* can only name three. Obviously, when the American media talk about "inclusiveness," they are not referring to the 42 percent of the American population that claim to be born again.

Finally, evangelicals can expect to be attacked through the American educational system.

An Attack on Education

It is now already the modus operandi of the public school system to attack God. Understand that the Supreme Court of the United States has already ruled it unconstitutional for the Ten Commandments to be posted on a class-

room wall. Why? Because it might affect the moral judg-
ments of students who read it and hence violate the separation of church and state.

You say, "This doesn't make sense. We need to have
someone who can do a better job articulating what we
believe. We need to explain why we should have a chance
to practice our faith without having that undermined. Is
this some new twisted logic? What's wrong? Why can't
they understand?"

The answer is this. They do understand. If someone has
determined that it is against the law to publicly post the Ten
Commandments in a classroom, a document whose historical and cultural impact on the world alone makes its words
some of the most important words in history, then no
amount of patient explanation will prevail. This isn't about
logic. This is about power, power to control the world,
power to control America, and power to control you!

When my son Matthew was in the second grade, he was
asked by his teacher to turn in a two-paragraph story on
Christmas in Mexico. He wrote about the wise men pursu-
ing the Christ child. The teacher rejected his paper because
the word *Christ* was mentioned. You can be sure Matthew's
father went to the schoolhouse and got that ludicrous decision rescinded.

The National Education Association, which controls education in America, was funded by the Rockefeller Foundation,
and the NEA has made it pretty clear that one of it's objectives for education in America is to get God out of the
schools. This is not something that is coming. This is here.
You can read *The Satanic Bible* in public school but not the
Ten Commandments. This is America in these latter days.

There is a strange irony here. Former communist leaders
are now coming to America and inviting Christians to go to
the Soviet Union to put together Christian education
blocks because they're trying to repair the massive moral
damage brought about by atheism. Meanwhile the Supreme
Court of the United States and the ACLU are insisting that

a new generation of young Americans must now try what has already failed in the former Soviet Union. Freedom of religion and freedom from religion is the difference between democracy and dictatorship. Which rules America?

You don't have to be a rocket scientist to know that when the Ten Commandments are thrown out and condoms are brought in, we're going the wrong way. Isn't it strange that a teacher cannot by law give your daughter an aspirin for a headache without a written letter of permission from you, her parents, but can counsel an abortion and even provide transportation to the clinic without ever telling you or giving you the right to talk to your own daughter.

Margaret Sanger who founded Planned Parenthood, which, not surprisingly, was also funded by the Rockefeller and Ford foundations, is given the unenviable sobriquet of the author of abortion in America. Her study called for unrestrained sexuality among America's teenagers. She then made the remarkable advocacy that all Jews, blacks, mental defectives, and religious and fundamental Christians be sterilized.[27] Her monograph *Breeding the Thoroughbred*, published in 1920 is a real eye–opener. If you want to know if the world loves you, semi-hates you, or totally hates you, read that. Yet Margaret Sanger is lionized by today's biased media who call you a bigot because you believe the Bible.

Those new by-words on American campuses and in American newsrooms, "politically correct," were coined fifty years ago. They translate simply as anti-God, anti-American, and pro-New World Order. It is nothing other than intellectual Nazism. Youngsters sent to secular universities are going to go through four years of intensive brainwashing and they're going to become secular humanists unless they are rooted in the sustaining power of the Word of God.

This is why Christian colleges and Christian universities

have to stay open in America. They help give this nation a chance to preserve its heritage and its faith.

Fourthly, before the rise of the New World Order in America, there must be the destruction of the traditional family.

The Attack on the Family

This process is also already upon us. The traditional family in America is coming unraveled. Increasingly, the objective of the state is to remove the authority of the parent from the child. If you've ever read the objectives of the United Nation's International Year of the Child, you will have no doubt of their intentions.[28]

Consider this: The same system that will allow a young lady injured in an automobile accident to suffer and bleed in a waiting room without anesthetic or treatment until parents are notified and have physically signed for a life-saving operation, will fearlessly and quickly kill her baby without any advice or input, or even without her parents knowing. All of this is justified, they say, because of the increase in teenage pregnancies. The parents haven't been able to solve the problem so, "We, the state, will do it for you."

You say, "Well, it hasn't worked. Teenage pregnancies are rising with the added bonus of epidemic venereal disease. Bring the parents back into the equation. Let us share our values with our children without undermining us by issuing programs and policies that contradict what we believe and are trying to teach to our children at home." Our children belong to us . . . not the government! You are perplexed and you wonder why the school boards and the teachers unions can't see the obvious. That's because you are still under a delusion. You think that you are part of a great public debate about what is best for your children. You imagine that the right argument will work. They will see the logic and change their minds. You are deceived. This isn't about logic. It isn't about what is best for your children. It's about power, power to train your child to abandon Judeo-Christian beliefs and become a submissive dupe to the New World Order.

How valuable is a high school diploma today? Boston University President John Silber states, "What a high school diploma tells you is that a student was *institutionalized* for about twelve years. You wouldn't know whether the student had been in a prison colony, a reform school, or a place for mental defectives."[29]

A Boston radio talk show host saw his ratings soar when he conducted an on-air no-holds-barred sex survey for women. Callers fought for the opportunity to do a psychic striptease by describing their favorite locations for intercourse (answers included against a chain link fence and on top of a washing machine), preferred positions, homosexual encounters, and the date when they lost their virginity.[30]

The soul of America is sick. Recently in New York City, dozens of motorists stopped to gawk, but made no move to intervene, while a man allegedly raped his three-year-old neice. Perhaps they thought they were watching the live production of a soap opera? [31]

In the past thirty years, the minds of our children have been vacuumed and sanitized. They have been poisoned against God. They have been poisoned against America. And the founding fathers of our nation are now being presented as lust-driven lunatics and as opportunists and non-patriots. In some classes more time is spent speculating on unproved, revisionist theories of Thomas Jefferson's alleged mistress than on the very lofty Jeffersonian principles that form the basis of our Bill of Rights. Seventy-five percent of America's high school graduates cannot give you the names of the last three presidents of these United States.

Woodrow Wilson said, "There is a power so organized in America, so subtle, so watchful, so pervasive, so interlocked that you better not speak about it above a whisper when you speak in condemnation of it."[32] The president of the United States was speaking of the clique of financiers and bankers who controlled America in his day. During our generation they rule from the Council on Foreign Relations.

During the last fifty years the Council on Foreign Relations has subtly co-opted or seized control of the U.S. State Department, the Treasury, the Federal Reserve, the Rockefeller, Ford, and Carnegie foundations, Harvard, Columbia, Yale, scores of international corporations, and every major media outlet in America. Since 1940, every secretary of state except one has come from this exclusive club. Is the picture beginning to focus for you?

They're trying to produce a one-world government that will kick God out. They see you as a nuisance and the only way they can neutralize you is to attack and reshape your image into one seen as totally counterproductive to progress in these United States.

The Last Warning

If one accepts the biblical timetable, someday soon Satan's messiah will present himself. Most Bible scholars expect him to emerge somewhere out of the European Economic Community. The ancient prophet Daniel gives a very clear description of a last days European Union reconstructed out of the nations of the Roman Empire of long ago. Daniel describes ten nations coming together in this union, with three of the smaller nations actually merging into one state.[33] Even as you read this book such an idea is being pushed by politicians and bankers in the nations of Belgium, the Netherlands, and Luxembourg. Many Europeans are already calling it Benelux.

The rise of the Antichrist will be sudden. In one single hour this new European Union will do its deed, signing over their legislative and bureaucratic powers to this new dictator who will be universally acclaimed as the world's best hope. The Bible says that in that hour the whole world will marvel and follow after him.[34]

People have told me, "Well that's impossible. It will not fall into place that quickly." Only a few years ago, learned history professors were teaching that this was the age of communism. Former Secretary of State Henry Kissinger caused a scandal when a Canadian journalist overheard him whisper to a dinner guest that the Soviet Union was in the ascendancy and the American era was over. Political science teachers were telling students that it would take a hundred years for the Berlin Wall to come down. But when God gave it a swift kick it came tumbling down in one evening. And understand, God, Himself, is going to allow these events to take place.

The Bible offers a detailed description of Satan's messiah. He will appear on the world's stage as a man of peace. "He shall cause craft to prosper."[34] After a collapse of the world's monetary system, he will assume control and usher in a few years of unprecedented and spectacular prosperity and peace.

Eventually, he will have a mystical or spiritual following. The Bible says that he will be "wounded in the head" and yet he will miraculously recover. He will have a New Age following. A great religious leader, described in the Bible as the false prophet,[36] will influence all organized religion to unite. "Why do we need Christ?" people will ask. "Haven't millions of people died fighting over Christ? Here is a man of peace. We have it all right here. He has even been assassinated and come back from the dead. What more could you ask?"

The Antichrist will even tackle the centuries-old problems of the Middle East. His solutions will appear miraculous and cause the world to "wonder after him." It will please the Arabs and, at the same time, guarantee the security of Israel by a seven-year peace treaty. But don't be deceived. The same prophets who say he will parade publicly as a man of peace, warn privately that he is, in fact, a beast, the Son of Perdition, meaning the "Chief Son of Satan."

The prophets declare that in the last days, Solomon's Temple, the ancient Seventh Wonder of the World, will be rebuilt. In the middle of his treaty with Israel, after three-and-a-half years of peace, the Antichrist will go to Jerusalem and walk into the Temple and formally announce to the people of the world what so many of them had already been saying. "You want God? All right, you've got him. I am God."

This is the climactic moment of the ages. Daniel writes about it. John writes about it. The Bible calls it "the abomination of desolation." Jesus said to those who see it happen, "Run to the mountains."[37] Don't even pack your bags. Run. It will be the last sign. There will be no other warning. And you will have very little time. It will trigger a period of unprecedented horrors. Even as the Antichrist is appearing as the man of peace—the fulfillment of John Lennon's famous song, uniting the world's religions, ending all wars—he will be betraying Israel, offering her up to her enemies for slaughter and extermination.

The Bible describes a two-hundred-million man army from "the East," which will close in on Jerusalem. Consider this, these remarkable words were prophesied at a time when the entire population of the world was only 250 million. Only today, in our lifetime, has any nation ever been able to claim a two-hundred-million man army. That is the exact number of the combined standing army and militia of the Peoples Republic of China. John Barron in his remarkable book *Operation Solo* writes about how the Chinese leaders often expressed the advantages of a nuclear war. "China would emerge the winner," they said, "because China has people in abundance. It is our one advantage."[38] They may get their wish.

War will break out upon the earth. It will not be just any war. It will be the ultimate expression of man's violence to man, ironically occurring just as mankind thought it had solved its problems. One prophet calls it "The Great Tribulation." The Bible's vivid descriptions are horrific. It is hard to imagine it as anything other than a nuclear holocaust. One third of the earth's living creatures and plants will be destroyed. One third of all life in the seas will be contaminated.

Whatever the Jewish people may think of Jesus, at that moment, many will take his advice. They will run to the mountains, hiding in a place among the cliffs called Petra. There, in horror, they will await their messiah, their deliverer. The Antichrist will finally set himself up as the object of worship in the city of Jerusalem. The Bible says, "He opened his mouth to blaspheme God."[39]

Literally, the Antichrist, Satan's messiah, is going to look into the heavens and he's going to say to the angels, "Had you followed me, had you followed my master, lord Satan when he was kicked out of the heavens, you would have controlled these kingdoms of the world with me."

The Second Coming

That blasphemy, that ultimate challenge mixed with the cries of His chosen people trembling with terror in the rocks of Petra, is the defining moment of the ages. Jesus will return to the Mount of Olives in Jerusalem. It will be the same spot from which he ascended into heaven 2,000 years ago. And this time he will be back with an army of angels and the raptured, resurrected church of the Lord Jesus Christ.

John describes it best in Revelation 19:11–21:

Then I saw Heaven opened, and behold, a white horse. And He who sat on him was called Faithful and True, and in righteousness He judges and makes war. His eyes were like a flame of fire, and on His head were many crowns. He had a name written that no one knew except Himself. He was clothed in a robe dipped in blood, and His name is called

The Word of God. And the armies in heaven, clothed in fine linen, white and clean, followed Him on white horses . . . And He has on His robe and on His thigh a name written KING OF KINGS AND LORD OF LORDS . . . Then the beast was captured, and with him the false prophet who worked signs in his presence . . . These two were cast alive into the lake of fire burning with brimstone.

So there are two world orders just ahead. One is led by Satan's messiah. The other is led by the true Messiah, Jesus Christ. You are likely to be a part of one of them. Paul said you're either servant to the Lord Jesus Christ or a slave to sin and Satan.

Some who actually read this book may very well receive that famous "mark of the beast," the number stamped on their forehead or right hand. They will be deceived. They have rejected the Word of God. They have rejected Jesus Christ. God has no place in their family. They are literally awaiting the messiah who will come out of Europe to destroy their family and their soul. They will say to themselves, "I have no choice. I cannot buy or sell without it." And when they receive it they will lose their soul for eternity.

Some who read this book will see the return of Jesus Christ. He will set up His throne in the city of Jerusalem. The first time He came as a baby wrapped in swaddling clothes, lying in a manger. The next time He comes, "He'll be wearing a crown and He shall be called the King of Kings and the Lord of Lords and of His kingdom, there shall be no end!"

The first time He came into Jerusalem he was riding on a donkey. The next time He will come in the final world order. He'll be riding a white horse followed by the armies of Heaven. It will be the greatest mounted posse ever to split the clouds.

The first time He came into Jerusalem He was dragged

before Pilot and Herod. Soldiers whipped Him and spit on Him. The next time He comes Herod and Pilot will be dragged before Him. Adolf Hitler will be dragged before Him. Joseph Stalin will bow. Nikita Khruschev will bow. Jean Paul Sarte, who long ago predicted the Bible would soon only be found only in museums, will bow. Professor Theodore Altizer, who declared in 1989 that "God is Dead," will bow. Doctor Death, Jack Kevorkian, will bow. Scientist Carl Sagan will bow. David Rockefeller will bow. The Bible says that "Every knee shall bow and every tongue shall confess that He is Lord."

The first time He came He was crucified at Calvary. The next time He comes He's going to reign on the throne of His father, David. You've heard of New Delhi, of New Brunswick, of New York. Well, according to the prophets of long ago, Jesus will reign in a "New Jerusalem." The governors and rulers of His kingdom will come and go from there. The truth of the Word of God that Jesus is the Lord to the glory of God the Father will be proclaimed from Zion's hill.

Don't be deceived by what is happening in America. Don't be perplexed by the outrageous actions of your government, by the injustice of the media, by the confusing economic signals. Jesus once gave this warning and this promise. "In the world, you will have tribulation, but be of good cheer, I have overcome the world."

Chapter 4

Land of the Free?

Most Americans have a vague, uncomfortable feeling that the freedom and justice we once took for granted in this country is slowly slipping away, but few are aware of how quickly that slippage has taken on landslide proportions. If you still think you live in an America where the people have the power, their vote determines their destiny, and the right to own property is inviolable, then you have missed a few key episodes of the evening news. You are deceived.

Consider for example, the rise of the homosexual lobby and its power to impose its agenda against popular opinion and the will of the people. Students at public schools in Massachusetts were ordered to perform in a "gay skit." Girls were directed to hold hands and act out the parts of lesbians. One boy had the line, "It's natural to be attracted to the same sex." In Boston a first grader came home telling his father that boys could become girls if they wanted to. The school had invited a transsexual to give the first graders a little education into life.

In Newton, Massachusetts, a parent decided to get involved. Teachers in the seventh grade were giving their classes graphic illustrations of oral and anal sex, but when Brian Camenker showed up at the school office asking to see the curriculum he was met by the principal and given a flat, "No."

"But statutory law gives parents the right to view curricula."

"Tough luck," he was told. "If you don't like it, take your kids to a private school."

Which is exactly what many parents of Massachusetts have done. Private school districts in Boston comprise some of the largest in the country and rival the public school system in the city. Parents who pay tuition at the private schools and property taxes supporting the public schools, get hit twice. But poorer families don't have that option. The withdrawal of thousands of caring parents from the public school system has only accelerated the move toward the new gay agenda. Those left behind often feel abandoned and are left to deal with the outrageous co-opting of the public educational system by a political lobby born in the bowels of hell.

In 1990, thousands of people in Colorado became alarmed by the growing homosexual lobby in their state. The lobby was pressuring local school boards to distribute pro-homosexual materials in classrooms and convincing state legislators to jump onto the gay legislative bandwagon. Not wanting to see a repeat of the Massachusetts mess in their own state, delegations of citizens visited their representatives. One of the entrenched, liberal, incumbent congressmen openly laughed at them. Meanwhile, some local state legislators privately encouraged citizens groups to get organized and warned them that if there was no opposition to the "gay" lobby the state would be steam-rolled.

At the same time several Colorado municipalities were pressured into passing pro-gay ordinances, which granted homosexuals "minority status." The door was open for gays to claim bias if they were denied employment, housing, health, and welfare services. Christian schools were now fearful that they would be required to hire gay teachers and be taken to court if they didn't. Christian landlords faced the same dilemma. Businesses could be sued if they could not show that they had hired their quota of gay workers.

Opposition leaders argued that minority status was granted to blacks and other groups for unique reasons that had no application in the gay community. Minorities were defined by the courts as having experienced economic disadvantages because of their race. For 150 years many American blacks had been slaves. Gays, on the other hand, earned far more than the average American, were three times more likely to be an airline frequent flyer, and had, on average, much more education than the norm. Why should minority status be granted to someone based on their choice of behavior? How could minority status be granted when the very same group was still outlawed by many state laws?

In 1992, groups of Colorado citizens set out to legally amend their state constitution. In spite of what you may have read in the press, no citizen of Colorado was advocating that homosexuals be denied the same freedoms any other American enjoys. The referendum simply stated that homosexuality and bisexuality could not be the basis to claim minority status or quota preferences. It was a very benign initiative, and purposely so. If this wouldn't pass, the homosexual lobby would own the state.

Thousands of citizens obtained the petitions, verified the signatures, overcame purposely misleading news stories spread by a hostile media, and successfully placed their initiative on the ballot. Now it was in the hands of the voters, or so they naively assumed.

Of course, Colorado voters overwhelmingly passed the initiative. In spite of daily newspaper attacks, it was never in doubt. National independent polling shows that six-out-of-ten Americans disapprove of gay marriages and gay adoptions even if it does buck the trends of Hollywood policy and American newsrooms.

The national media were outraged. This wasn't politically correct. Hollywood magnates and gay activists leaders called for a Colorado boycott to punish the voters. Attempts to explain what was really going on in the state were panned.

And then, it happened. Judicial reversal. The Supreme Court of the United States, which in 1986 had upheld state laws making homosexual acts criminal offenses, now told the people of Colorado they could not even amend their own state constitution. Their votes didn't count. Their concerns for their children and their beliefs didn't count. The same Supreme Court that outlawed the posting of the Ten Commandments in a public classroom in Tennessee and ordered a manger scene pulled off the lawn of a city courthouse in Connecticut was now telling the people of Colorado that the laws they passed, even the constitutional changes they made, would have to fit the dictates of a politically correct, Satan-inspired, homosexual agenda. Don't be deceived. America is no longer a free country whose destiny is determined by citizens voting their beliefs. America's destiny is being determined by activist federal judges who are beyond the reach of the election process. It is a government by fiat! It's time for federal judges to face the ballot box. To believe activist federal judges will allow the citizens of America to live by any conviction they don't condone is deception.

But the assault didn't end there.

A Godless Government

In 1993, a new American president legitimized homosexuality by demanding that they be accepted into the military. God calls it sodomy, an abomination. Sodomy is a sin. One is not born that way. It is a choice. In his first week in office the new president made it clear that the abortion mills would continue the genocide of millions of babies. Within days he had announced a new surgeon general of the United States who, among other things, encouraged the idea that grade school children be taught how to masturbate as a form of "sex control." Yet millions of born-again

Christians continue to support this president and other politicians because "the economy is strong." Mammon wins over morality.

A politician who carries a Bible before crowds and television cameras does not make a godly man. Attending church once a week does not make a godly man. A politician who goes to the White House and is sworn in with his right hand on the Bible, while his left hand is signing documents that federally fund partial-birth abortions, is not a godly man. God does not judge mankind on style, only on substance. As a people, we have been deceived by symbolism over substance.

Today, as a direct result of that loss of discernment, America has its most wicked, evil, and dangerous leadership in its 220-year history. It is a leadership saturated with socialist, Marxist, gay, and lesbian ideals. America's new elitists seek to destroy America's Constitution. They lead a constant assault against traditional family values, the religious heritage of our nation, and a free-enterprise economy. They are a self-serving, politically correct crowd, using the politics of hate and class warfare to undermine our basic principles.

The result?

The process begun by activist judges in the 1960s has become an avalanche. America is a sick society! Our children are deluged with daily messages of "safe sex," which have only encouraged promiscuity. Children in fifth-grade classrooms are passed a banana and shown how to put on a condom. America has one-million teenage pregnancies each year. Half of the female teenage population is sexually active between the ages of fifteen and nineteen. Sixty percent of black children are born out of wedlock. By the year 2000, if the present rate of illegitimacy continues, the government projects that 60 percent of all children born will be illegitimate.

Abortion has only accelerated the idea that life is cheap. We read daily headlines of drive-by shootings, recreational murders, and women who are being raped at a rate of one every forty-eight seconds. Prime-time television now glorifies profanity and nudity.

"Professing to be wise, they became fools." Meanwhile, America's educational system is in disarray. Thousands of children carry guns to public schools. Teachers are assaulted by students on a daily basis. The classroom, once a center for learning, has become a center for governmental mind control. Secular humanist educators continue to poison the minds of our innocent children.

The Village Wants Your Children

Hillary Clinton has written her book, *It Takes A Village*. The idea is that none of us can make it alone. We need the village, with its various talents and protections. Sounds good, doesn't it? And according to Hillary Clinton, it is impossible to raise a child without the help of the village. Insert the words *big government* for *village* and you have Hillary's concept.

Childrearing is a tough business, especially if the mother is off doing something truly fulfilling with her life, like becoming a lawyer and promoting liberal causes to advance humanity.

Oh yes, children have rights too. That's part of the formula. In fact, children should have the same rights as parents. A child should be able to divorce his or her parents. Children do not belong to parents, they belong to the village, and sometimes the village has to take them away. Sometimes their needs supersede the needs of the parents. Hillary Clinton calls such a society "a village" but the trend is not new; it has been underway in this country for thirty years. And it is not a village. It is an all-powerful government dictating to parents what they can and cannot do with their own children.

A third-grade teacher in East Lansing, Michigan, decided on her own that a young male student was too shy. He needed "a friend." Without the parents knowledge or permission, she ordered him into psychological therapy sessions with a counselor. When the parents learned of the action and objected, a negotiation ensued. The parents finally agreed that their son could "play games" and chat with the counselor. They imagined a friendly conversation over a game of Chinese Checkers. They assumed the counselor was a professional. Surely, the village is that competent.

Within a week the boy began to show signs of severe emotional problems. The parents became alarmed and started asking questions about the school therapy sessions. They were told in no uncertain terms to "butt out." Such sessions are "confidential." The boy was given strict instructions not to tell his parents what the sessions were all about. Understand, you don't own your child. The village owns your child.

When the boy's problems became worse, they took him to a psychiatric doctor of their own choosing. He concluded that the boy had "separation anxiety disorder and panic attacks." Something at school was only aggravating a serious problem. The parents, unable to get the school to respond or even reveal what was going on in the secret sessions with their child, took the school to court. In fact, it went all the way to the Supreme Court. In the process they learned that the boy's counselor was not a professional, he had only taken a few undergraduate psychology courses. The game he was playing with the boy was called, "The Talking, Feeling, and Doing Game." It had been recommended by the music teacher. I'll leave it to your imagination to figure out what was going on. The parents charged that they had been deprived of their parental rights to raise their child and properly watch over his medical well-being.[1]

Of course, going to court in these United States is the last place one will find justice. The U.S. District Court naturally sided with the school and the Supreme Court refused to hear it. In a related case, Texas judge Melinda Harmon ruled that, "Parents give up their rights when they drop the children off at public school."

And that's only one case. Believe me there are others as disturbing. In March of 1996 fifty young girls in an East Stroudsburg, Pennsylvania, intermediate school were given genital examinations. The girls were forced to disrobe and stand in line while a female pediatrician gave the exams. She said she was looking for genital warts.

Mrs. Kate Tucker, mother of one of the eleven-year-old girls, said that the pediatrician had them "lie down on a table, spread-eagled, with nothing covering them." The daughter said the exam was given despite her pleas to call her parents. Many of the girls were crying and trying to get out the door, which was barred by a nurse. It takes a village, folks.

"My mother wouldn't like this," one of the girls said, "I'd like to call her." She was told, "No." The girl then calmly said that she didn't want the test done. "Too bad," the nurse responded. The doctor refused to talk to the girls or offer any explanation for the examinations.

Parents felt helpless and then enraged. They learned that Pennsylvania State health guidelines require public schools to notify parents and urge them to attend medical exams. Still, nothing was done; no apology was given. The school district investigated and decided that there were no improprieties.[2] After all, the children don't belong to the parents. They belong to the village, and if the village wants to take a look, they can do it. Remember what the court says, "Parents give up their rights when they drop the children off at public school."

One thing is for sure, we may no longer be the land of the free, but we still are very much the home of the brave. It takes courage for parents and children to survive in this jungle they call "a village" in these latter days.

The NEA Takeover

Some villagers are more favored than others in the New America, and no one is more favored than the National Education Association. The NEA is the nation's largest teacher's union with more than 2.2 million members. While the organization is highly political and partisan it has been given a special "national charter" by Congress, exempting it from more than $16 million in real estate taxes, money which would normally go to help the local public schools. This "national charter" is the same status given to the Red Cross, but I guarantee you, the NEA is not in the business of educating your children. They are nothing but a tax-funded, liberal, political lobby that could care less about educational excellence in America.

In the past decade, the NEA has taken up the fight to separate children from their parents. You could call it "Village Empowerment." Former NEA president Keith Geiger, and both candidates seeking to replace him, think parent involvement takes away from a teacher's authority and, thus, schools must be "protected."

While the NEA led the fight to strip the Christian Coalition of its non-profit status for engaging in "partisan politics," the NEA has hypocritically and blatantly displayed its power by its open partisan agenda. In the 1996 election cycle, the NEA spent $5.5 million in political action committee (PAC) funds to elect liberal politicians and defend the liberal agenda, plus another $20.7 million on training members for political campaign work and lobbying. Out of 235 candidates endorsed by them in the 1996 election, only one Republican was given any money.[1] The NEA is openly using compulsory union dues and millions of dollars in federal grants to support a liberal political agenda.

In seeking to eliminate stereotyping and discrimination, NEA resolution B-7 decided that homosexuality should be listed in the same category with race, gender, immigration status, physical disabilities, and ethnic origins. The idea is that people are born gay and lesbian; they have no choice in the matter and so their practices and behavior must be accepted. It doesn't matter what the Bible says. Incidentally, there is no mention or concern about religious stereotyping or discrimination.

Resolution B-7 is a follow-up to resolution B-9, passed at the 1995 NEA convention. B-9 requires positive plans and ongoing training programs to teach about "homosexuals throughout history," promote acceptance of "diverse sexual orientation," and celebrate "Lesbian and Gay History Month."

Now, let me give you a little bit of good news in the midst of this thunderstorm of decadence. Resolution B-9 was rendered ineffective after an outcry from Christian parents. Twelve NEA state affiliates condemned it and numerous teachers around the country resigned from the NEA in protest. The vast majority of teachers refused to participate in "Gay History Month." Don't be deceived. Things are bad, but they would be even worse if godly influence was totally withdrawn from this country. The answer is not to run off and hide in a cave somewhere. The answer is to stand up and expose the darkness. The answer is to be salt and light in these days of decadence and deception

Even so, the new resolution B-7 is even more dangerous than its predecessor. The same objectives of promoting the gay and lesbian lifestyle are all there, but now they are hidden amid honorable programs for minorities and the handicapped. Those who speak out are labeled racist, insensitive, intolerant, homophobic, right-wing, Bible-believing hate mongers.

There is nothing that the NEA fears more than a voucher system, a tax credit that would allow parents to enroll their children in a school of their choice. They know what would happen. Many parents would take their vouchers to

Christian schools. And if that was prohibited by the courts, as it most surely would be, they would at least enroll their children in schools that teach more educational basics and less liberal political dogma.

In recent years the public clamor for a voucher system has reached a crescendo. The NEA and Bill Clinton have suddenly teamed up, declaring themselves as born-again proponents of the popular idea. Again, don't be deceived. The new charter schools of Clinton and the NEA will be exclusively non-religious and far more liberal and experimental than anything ever seen in a public school that has had some measure of accountability.

One part of the new look of education is "out-based" education.

Out-Based Education

In recent years, our educational leaders have seized on a new system called out-based education, commonly called OBE. Its mission is to eliminate academic competition from the classroom. There will be no grades. There will be no year-end accomplishments. No one will fail. And no one will succeed or receive honors. To receive an honor might offend those who received no honor . . . unthinkable! All super-achievers must be dumbed down so the mainstream students can feel better about themselves. This will supposedly restore self-esteem and encourage a community spirit. OBE will not teach subjects such as reading, writing, and arithmetic; instead they will teach attitudes, environmentalism, global citizenship, and multiculturalism.

The rest of the world is teaching their students math and science while in America we're teaching our children to get in touch with their inner selves. Moreover, the student's "attitude" will be evaluated by the teacher and if a child has a "politically incorrect" attitude, he or she will be denied a diploma. Ironically, the only failure allowed will be ideological. They even propose that all businesses contact the school before hiring a graduate to be sure the student has a "politically correct" attitude before getting a job. Hello, New World Order!

So far, America's new secular, anti-Christian campaign has not led to the intellectualism some anticipated. No government or laws can inhibit man's intuitive search for the spiritual world beyond. But instead of seeking God's wisdom, the "New Age" religions search for spiritual answers from alien beings, fortune tellers, and demons. Environmental pagans are now worshiping Mother Earth. Increasingly they call on Gaia, the ancient earth goddess who is only a recycled version of Baal, the pagan god of biblical history.

A little-known fact about these fanatical environmentalists is that they consider Christians to be the enemy. Environmentalist Lynn White, Jr. advocated that a worsening ecological crisis would continue until Americans rejected the Christian axiom that nature has no reason for existence except to serve man.

God said, "Let us make man in Our image, according to Our likeness; let them have dominion over the fish in the sea, over the birds in the air, over the cattle, over all the earth and over every creeping thing that moves on the earth."[2] This paragraph offers God's perspective of exactly why the physical world was created. It was created for the benefit of all mankind. And as the benefactors of the earth, mankind has a very real responsibility for nurturing this great gift from God; but God is above nature and the earth is the Lord's.

The Collapse of Moral Law

The book of Isaiah speaks about a time when people will seek for justice and not find it. That time is here for America. Our courts, once held up to the world as examples of justice and fairness, are now the object of scorn and mistrust. Right and wrong no longer matter.

In America, celebrities commit murder and walk while first graders are expelled for kissing. Our priorities are sick! God has been abandoned in American public life and with Him any belief in absolutes of right and wrong. Wrong is only what the state says is wrong; it does not exist on its own. Thus the question no longer is, "Did this man rape and murder the little girl?" Even if we know the answer to that question—even if the jury knows the answer—it isn't enough. The important questions are now, "Was the accused apprised of his rights? Was the police paperwork done correctly?" If not, he can go. In the absence of moral law we are only left with procedure.

The government's own statistics show that 6 percent of all violent criminals commit more than 70 percent of all violent crimes. The same people are committing their crimes over and over as liberal judges release them to attack taxpaying citizens over and over like packs of ravenous wolves. In fact, half of all suspects charged with a violent crime will be returned to the streets even before their trial begins. During this time, 20 percent of them will escape and 16 percent will commit another crime, even before they have been tried for the first one.[3] Justice delayed is justice denied!

Even more shocking are the vast numbers of criminals caught in the act who are simply let loose without a trial. For every one hundred serious crimes committed in this country only five criminals will go to jail.

Typical was the experience of New York police officers in a celebrated drug bust that happened in broad daylight on the streets of the city. The officers were cruising a well-known drug area at five in the morning when they became suspicious of a slow-moving automobile with out-of-state license plates. The car stopped and four men appeared with two large duffel bags that were thrown into the trunk of the vehicle. When the police approached the car, the men fled in opposite directions.

Some of the men and the driver, a woman, were appre-hended. Inside the open trunk police found eighty pounds of cocaine. Now, these were not novice policemen. They had already experienced their fair share of cases thrown out of court on technicalities. The officers were very care-ful to advise the suspects of their rights under the Miranda ruling of the Supreme Court. Even so, the driver openly confessed on videotape saying that this was just one of a number of drug buys made that very day in the city.

The prosecutor's office was ecstatic. This time the police officers had done everything right. Their pursuit was war-ranted; after all, the suspects had fled. Their search passed the stringent "probable cause" requirement, which prohibits a policeman from searching you or your vehicle without a reason. They had witnessed the men throwing duffel bags in the trunk of their car; in fact that action had precipitated their flight. The trunk was open. Best of all they had read the suspects their Miranda rights, they had confessed any-way, and all of it had been captured on videotape.

The predictable happened anyway. Federal judge Harold Baer, a Clinton appointee, dismissed the case announcing to a shocked courtroom that the police search was unrea-sonable after all. Since policemen in the neighborhood were generally regarded as corrupt it was a natural reaction for the men to flee and thus was unreasonable for the police to be suspicious. As columnist John Leo said, the criminals had the right to suspect the police but the police didn't have the right to suspect the criminals!

I love America. I believe God has blessed her for her orig-inal covenant with Him. It is my prayer and hope that America will awaken to the Words of God and turn back to Him. But if you still operate under the illusion that this is the land of "life, liberty, and justice for all," you are deceived.

If you need more evidence, consider these cases:

- A three-judge panel on a U.S. Circuit Court reversed a conviction against a would-be bomber trying to kill the

U.S. attorney who had once prosecuted him. The court determined that the bomb had been badly built and could not, therefore, be considered deadly or dangerous. Case dismissed.

- A young woman, seeking protection from an abusive ex-boyfriend, was unlucky enough to find herself in the New York court room of judge Lorin Duckman. The ex-boyfriend, a convicted rapist, had already attacked the young lady three times. After commenting that the woman was bruised but not actually disfigured, the judge lowered bail for the man. He advised the woman that her former boyfriend would probably stop beating her if she would just give him back his dog. Before the end of the month the former boyfriend had shot the woman to death.

- Judge Rosemary Barkett, a typical Clinton appointee, opposed Georgia state laws requiring candidates to be tested for drugs. She said it was unfair. It would be prejudicial to candidates who favored legalizing drugs. While a member of the Florida Supreme Court she insisted that police be stopped from searching for drugs on public buses, even with permission from the passengers. She now sits on the U.S. Court of Appeals.

Without God, without absolutes, without a belief in right or wrong, justice in these United States has been reduced to a game of regulations. Morality does not exist outside of the law. Guilt and innocence do not exist outside the law. And the law is no longer in the hands of the citizens. Corrupt, activist judges now hold the power. The law is what they decide it will be, and that can change by the hour.

In Cleveland, Ohio, a nineteen-year-old woman was ready to plead guilty to credit card abuse before judge Shirley Strickland Saffold. Before accepting the plea, Saffold began a lengthy lecture. "Men are easy," she said.

"You can go sit in the bus stop, put on a skirt, cross your legs, and pick up twenty-five. Ten of them will give you money. If you don't pick up the first ten," the judge solemnly advised, "then all you got (sic) to do is open your legs a little bit and cross them at the bottom, and then they'll stop." The judge suggested that the young woman find a doctor and marry him. This would solve her financial problems.⁴ Welcome to justice in America. Welcome to America without God.

The prophet Isaiah wrote, "He brings the princes to nothing; He makes the judges of the earth useless."⁴

Agencies of Injustice

In the Bible, David talked about justice turned upside-down, when right is wrong and wrong is right. Sound familiar? While the guilty freely walk the streets of America, the innocent are often successfully prosecuted and harassed by a government that has lost a belief in right and wrong and is solely driven by rules and regulations.

A man living in Knoxville, Tennessee, saved $3.33 by mailing his tax form to the IRS by regular mail. The small savings, however, turned into a tragic loss. James Carroll mailed his tax document to the Internal Revenue Service on January 21, 1987. It was due in March of the same year. Somehow the IRS did not receive the document, and although Mr. Carroll could prove he had sent it, he could not prove that the IRS had received it.

A 1916 common law, amended by Congress in 1954, seemed to support Mr. Carroll. The law stated that proof of a letter mailed, "creates a presumption that it reached its destination and was actually received." An updated 1954 amendment added that a record showing that a document had been sent by registered mail would constitute "prima facie evidence of delivery to the IRS."

It was now up to the Circuit Court of Appeals to interpret the amendment. What was the intent? Was it only adding the idea that the use of the new registered mail service would also be proof or was it actually negating the original law applying to regular mail? The 8th and 9th Circuit Courts, as well as the Tennessee Tax Court, had already sided with the original common law, "proof that the letter was mailed creates a presumption that it reached its destination and was actually received." But Mr. Carroll lived in the 2nd Circuit Court's district. It was their call.

What was lost in this whole discussion was the fact that Mr. Carroll was innocent. No one, not even the IRS, denied that. The question was purely technical. The 2nd Circuit Court decided that the old common law of presumption no longer applied and that Mr. Carroll was at fault for not having sent the tax information through the registered mail. An innocent man was fined $22,000 in late fees and court costs. That will teach you to use the U.S. mail. Welcome to the new style of justice in America in these latter days.

In 1988 Nobel Peace Prize recipient Mother Teresa and her Missionaries of Charity were given two abandoned buildings from the City of New York for a dollar bill. The sisters proposed to convert these buildings into homeless shelters. A year-and-a-half later, the city finally approved the plan and restoration began. But soon after efforts were underway, the Missionaries of Charity came face-to-face with the reality of trying to do something in the new America. The sisters were told that under New York's building code, all new or renovated multiple-story buildings were required to have, or install, an elevator. The Missionaries of Charity explained that because of their oath of poverty, they would never use the elevators and, in any case, they didn't have the extra money to put the elevators in.

Although there were thousands of buildings in New York City without elevators and the buildings given to the sisters were abandoned and unused, and although the missionaries simply wanted to provide food and shelter to the homeless, they were denied any waiver. The city took back its buildings. They are empty to this day! Better to have homeless people sleeping in the streets in snow than sleeping in a nice, warm bed in a building without elevators.

The Government and Your Property

Few Americans understand how important faith was to the founding of our country. The Mayflower Covenant was a covenant with God. Most of our Constitution and early amendments are rooted in Scripture. The Fifth Amendment, which clearly prohibits government from taking property without just compensation, is no exception. The Bible teaches that a man's property is sacred: "Do not remove the ancient landmark which your fathers have set."[5]

In 1964 Gaston and Monique Roberge began looking for a secure retirement investment, not an easy chore in an economy periodically given to bouts of rampaging inflation. They finally decided to invest in real estate, and their search lead them to a small, 2.8-acre plot near the banks of the Atlantic Ocean in Orchard Beach, Maine.

There they dreamed of a day when increased tourism and nearby development would increase the value of their land. By 1976 the area was indeed experiencing rapid growth. With development soaring, the city government asked the Roberges if one of their sewer contractors could dump excess dirt onto part of their land. It seemed to be a good idea. The Roberges wanted to be cooperative. The city would provide the permits and some of their marshy land would receive a much-needed land fill.

By 1986 with Orchard Beach thriving, Mr. Roberge's health was now in full decline. There had been two heart attacks and doctors were informing him that he was going to lose his sight. The Roberges decided it was time to sell. A developer quickly offered them top dollar for their property, planning to build condominiums on the area that had been land-filled ten years earlier. Orchard Beach officials approved the zoning. Mr. and Mrs. Roberge could finally cash in on their investment and start their long-awaited retirement.

But life is seldom that simple in these United States in these latter days. There was one more step. The federal government. And what did the federal government have to do with a small real estate transaction in the state of Maine, you may ask? The developer, sensitive to the growing regulatory role of the Environmental Protection Agency and the U.S. Army Corps of Engineers, wanted to make sure that everything was okay with them—just in case.

Sure enough, the Army Corps of Engineers decided that the small property could be technically categorized as "wetlands." An investigation ensued. The sale was postponed, and after five months of waiting the developer was finally denied permits to build. Investigators concluded that the land filled in by the sewer contractor ten years before was part of a marsh extending beyond the Roberge's property. The Corps insisted that federal permits should have been obtained before the land had been filled in. The city, of course, had initiated the project and had issued permits allowing the land to be filled. Everything was legal at the time, but now, retroactively, the Corps decided to hold the Roberge's accountable. To add to the absurdity of this tale, no federal agency even issued such permits ten years before. Preservation of wetlands was a political issue not yet born. At the time, the Roberges could not have obeyed such a regulation even if God, Himself, had shown them the future.

Now, belatedly, the Roberges filed for a federal permit. They were denied. They hired experts to assist in obtaining technical information for an "after the fact" permit, but that costly process was also in vain. New applications from the Roberges only prompted a continuous cycle of requests from the agency for additional information.

Eventually the Roberges found an attorney to work on consignment and a five-year legal battle began. Among other things, the attorneys discovered an existing internal policy that prohibited the pursuit of alleged violations more than five years old. This was something the agency understood—a regulation. The government finally issued the permits that should have been issued so many years before.

Then came the shocker. Further investigation revealed that the Corps had all the necessary information from the Roberges all along. Its refusal to issue the permits was inconsistent with standard practices. Additionally, they discovered that one man in the Corps had been responsible for the continued hassles and delays. He had been bored with his position and had been trying to "squash" the Roberges to set an example of the agency's power. Even so, no apologies were given and no one in the agency was disciplined. Welcome to the land of the free!

When the government fears its citizens you have democracy. When the citizens fear the government, you have tyranny. After Waco, Ruby Ridge, and Travelgate, Americans fear the government, and justly so.

Americans beware. Look to history as your warning. The psychic gods of Nazi Germany led to unspeakable horrors across Europe. It happened once; it can happen again! America's new atheist, secular state is not unprecedented. It was performed with precision by the Soviet Communists and led to an amoral, unproductive, cynical, and atheistic population that destroyed its own economy and is only now having to learn how to think and live freely. Even so, against all logic, America's leaders try to force upon us a system of government that has repeatedly failed in Europe and Russia. Why? There is no logical answer.

But, remember, this is not about logic. Logical people do not reject a political system that has given them freedom and prosperity. Logical people do not regress to the centuries-old worship of Baal. This is not about what is right or wrong for America. The other side doesn't even believe in right or wrong. This is about principalities, powers, and the rulers of darkness. America is in a spiritual crisis. This is a battle for America's soul, and while you may not be around to experience it at its climactic worst, your children and grandchildren will be there. The antichrist system is taking shape. America's future hangs in the balance in these latter days.

How to Fight Back Spiritually

There is good news in the midst of this depressing recital of America's woes. All power is from God. The Bible says, "Let every soul be subject to the governing authorities. For there is no authority except from God, and the authorities that exist are appointed by God."[6] Every politician, every judge, every policeman and king are servants of God. America's leaders are controlled by God.

Consider Daniel and King Nebuchadnezzar of Babylon. The king had a terrifying dream but had forgotten it. He commanded his witchcraft corps to tell him what he had dreamed or he would rip them limb-from-limb. Daniel, an Israelite captive trained as a wise man in the court, asked for time to pray about it. "The God whom we serve will give us the answer," he said. When God revealed the dream and the interpretation, Daniel announced, "Blessed be the name of God forever and ever, for wisdom and might are His."[7] God has all the might and all the power. "The King's heart is . . . like the rivers of water; He turns it wherever he wishes."[8]

Now here is the irony: Who controls the president's heart like water? God! Who controls the senators' hearts like water? God! And ultimately, the only Supreme Court that makes a difference is God. "For exhaltation comes neither from the east, nor the west, nor from the south. But God is the Judge: He puts one down, and exalts another."[9] America is not in the hands of politicians; the politicians are in the hands of God.

King Nebuchadnezzar of Babylon was having a massive government gala with a thousand of his lords, and they were mocking God. "They drank wine, and praised the gods of gold and silver, bronze and iron, wood and stone. In that same hour the fingers of a man's hand appeared and wrote opposite the lampstand on the plaster of the wall of the king's palace; and the king saw the part of the hand that wrote." The Bible says that his countenance changed. His thoughts troubled him so that "the joints of his hips were loosened and his knees knocked against each other."[10] The king was terrified. God scared the devil out of him.

They called for Daniel, and when he arrived he gave the interpretation. He told them God was saying that the kingdom was finished; they had been weighed in the balances and found wanting. This great world empire would be divided between the Medes and Persians.

That very night the Persians reversed the flow of a key tributary of the great Euphrates river and came in under the massive walls of Babylon. The king of Babylon was killed, and by morning the world had a new Persian ruler.

"All power is from God."

If God is in charge, why doesn't He do a better job of picking his leaders? you might ask.

The answer is simple. God has given to men the gift of free will. The choice is ours, not God's. The crisis that America is experiencing today is one that we, ourselves, have brought on our own heads. The elections are more about the character of the people than the candidates for office. When Israel journeyed through the desert, God sent them manna from heaven. No one cooked meals. No one did dishes. No one even had to pack up the leftovers in Tupperware. Manna was nutritious and God always sent enough for each day's need. Even so, the Israelites complained. They knew better than God. They wanted meat.

So God gave them their desire and sent the fowls to the Israelites, and Numbers [11] records that "while the meat was still between their teeth, before it was chewed," God killed them. One of the worst things that can happen to you is to get what you want. I believe God is saying to America, "How much corruption will you endure before you say 'Enough is enough'? How long will you endure evil under the banner of 'tolerance'? How long before you cry out for a revival of righteousness?"

The Israelites' story is the story of America. Our founding pilgrim fathers prayed for God's blessing. They stamped "In God We Trust" on their money. They declared a day of Thanksgiving as a national holiday so their children and grandchildren for generations would know what God had done for them. Harvard University was built by Puritans to educate their ministers to preach the gospel. Every school day began with a moment of prayer. Every session of Congress began with a prayer. And God blessed America with unprecedented prosperity and freedom. American cars filled the highways of Europe, Asia, and South America. Students came from every country to gain the prestige of a diploma from an American university. American medicine was the envy of the world. Our industrial power reached a crescendo during World War II burying Hitler's Nazis. Our farms prospered. America was feeding the world with its leftovers.

But in our power, in our strength, we grew proud and godless. We chose hedonism, humanism, and paganism as our new gods. It was not just a calculated decision of Hollywood. Born-again Christians voted by marching off to every *Friday the 13th* movie that came out. Our habits and tastes drove the machine. We chose pornography and promiscuity. We chose materialism and greed and selfishness that led to abortion and incest. In our permissiveness we created the vacuum for an aggressive, man-hating, lesbian-run, feminist movement. We wanted our children to like us, so we abandoned God's plan for the family and gave them what they wanted, and a savage, virulent form of teenage violence resulted.

The Bible is very clear. The Bible reminds us that we are not a part of this world. 1 John 2:15 warns "Do not love the world or the things in the world." Even so, we sought the world's opinion and favor more than the favor of our own creator. We tried to please the trendy appetites of a jaded and corrupt crowd of journalists. We sought the favor of an arrogant, godless, new breed of academia. Just as Satan used God's words to tempt Eve and to tempt Jesus, we used God's words to justify our compromises with a growing secular society. After all, the Bible says to live in peace. We showed the world that we weren't intolerant, Neanderthal, Christian cavemen. We could be "liberal." We voted in the governments that appointed anti-God judges. We voted in anti-God school boards and sat at home when they held their meetings. We fed the monster, and today we are its prisoner!

God responds to our choice—not His choice, our choice. Do you want to know what God is doing in heaven right now? He's looking down at us asking, "I wonder just how much filth they'll accept before they answer the wake-up call?"

Before pleading with God for intervention we must ask ourselves what we are doing to change things. We can fight back. We can make a difference. As a good steward do we exercise our right to vote? Do we petition government? How can we criticize if we have not confronted?

You say, "Well, what good will writing a letter do?" But our responsibility is to do our part, and the Bible teaches confrontation. The government is responsible before God for its reaction. Our church members in San Antonio have taken the lead on many community issues and have seen their work succeed. In one week more than 300,000 responded to our call to block federal bureaucratic guidelines that would have prevented workers from wearing a cross around their neck at the workplace. Republican

Senator Dole and Democrat Senator Heflin met with me and rushed into place a "mood of the Senate," warning the federal authorities that any such decision would be defeated by the Senate. The godless legislation died in the birth canal because the righteous stood up and spoke up. The Bible says: "Let the redeemed of the Lord, say so!"[11]

We are Americans! Heirs to pilgrim pioneers who looked to this land as a haven for freedom of worship. Heirs to founding fathers whose dreams will die if we give up. We must participate! And we must vote for the things that matter most, the character and integrity of the candidates. "Those who forsake the law praise the wicked, But such as keep the law contend with them."[12] We are in a war for the soul of this nation. Don't expect to be liked. Jesus said, "You will be despised by all men for my sake." Don't expect to get justice in the enemy's court. Don't expect to be praised in the enemy's newspapers. The future of America, of our children and grandchildren, is at stake and the price is freedom. It is time for God's people to stand up. It is time for God's people to speak up, to "contend" with the wicked. But be warned, the clock is ticking. It is late in the battle. This one will never be won by ballots alone. It will take a miracle.

Can we take America back? The answer is yes!

How? Through the power of prayer that God will send a mighty revival of righteousness to America—a revival of evangelism, traditional family values, morality, integrity, work ethic, and individual responsibility.

Take Our Country Back

I recently met with a born-again Christian who served two presidents of the United States. He worked on the White House senior staff, saw the president almost daily, and sometimes sat in on meetings with heads-of-state. "At first I saw Christian activism as the only solution," he told me. "But after watching how things work, I quickly realized that running a government was not that much different from running a family. Prayer is often more powerful than anything you can say or do."

The Bible echoes the wisdom of this statement:

- "Call to Me, and I will answer you, and show you great and mighty things, which you do not know."[13]
- "You do not have because you do not ask."[14]

The initiative rests with us, not with God. "Whatever you bind on earth will be bound in heaven, and whatever you loose on earth will be loosed in heaven."[15] I repeat, the initiative rests with us. Our prayers on earth determine what God will do in the heavens. Authority is given to be used and the church has the power of His name, His blood, and His Word. Jesus said to his disciples, "Behold, I give you the authority to trample on serpents and scorpions, and over all the power of the enemy, and nothing shall by any means hurt you."[16] We are told by the prophets and by Jesus that we have the power to go directly to Almighty God and that He will give us the desires of our hearts. Now that's power! But we must use it.

America's future is not in the hands of the ungodly, it is in the hands of God's children. It is up to us to seek God's help. "And you shall be to Me a kingdom of priests and a holy nation. These are the words which you speak to the children of Israel."[17]

When Nehemiah, cup bearer to King Xerxes, heard about the destruction of Jerusalem, he fell on his face before God and wept. He didn't apply for a government grant. He didn't seek an audience with the king. He understood how spiritual power works. He placed his need before the One who has all power in heaven and in earth and cried out to God for Jerusalem.

The king asked Nehemiah, "How are you? You look

sick." Nehemiah told the king his burden for Jerusalem and the king said, "I'll give you the timber, the money, and the time to go and rebuild the walls." One man, one prayer, and God moved a king's heart like water. That one prayer reshaped history.

When Israel was besieged by the vast Assyrian armies, the prayer of Hezekiah changed the course of battle. The angel of the Lord walked through the Assyrian camp and slew the thousands of men who the day before had openly mocked the God of Israel. He smote the sentries at their posts. He smote the officers as they rehearsed their battle plans and the rank and file as they slept in their tents. Suddenly and swiftly, the angel of the Lord moved through that camp leaving 185,000 dead Assyrians in his wake, and Israel was delivered from certain annihilation. Why? Because one man prayed one prayer and God answered him. One man's prayer shaped history. Now that's power!

And modern church history is filled with the same kinds of stories. Just after World War II, Joseph Stalin revealed to a few trusted staffers that he was going to execute the Jews of Russia. When word eventually leaked out of the country, the believers in England began to fast and pray for God to save the Jews. At the end of the twelfth day, Stalin had a brain hemorrhage. Sixteen doctors worked to no avail; he died and the Jews were saved. There is the power of prayer!

Ask yourself, if the prayer of one man like Hezekiah or Nehemiah can make a difference, what would happen if thousands of American Christians began praying for a revival of righteousness in our country? Prayer is the most powerful tool we have; it is our direct link to God. It is "access." Understand, God is not a genie in a bottle. He cannot be sent forth to run our errands or make our fantasies come true. But prayer does release His power on our enemies, our accusers, our sick bodies, or on the Prince of Darkness. But as powerful as God is, He cannot answer prayers that are not prayed.

Do you love America? Pray! Do you love your children?

Pray! We must accept this responsibility or we will suffer the consequences.

When the crisis was upon us in the 1960s, thousands of Christians prayed and fasted and for a brief time the drift away from God was stemmed. God is waiting for the church of the twenty-first century to answer His wake-up call. He is waiting for us to once more take a stand against evil with prayer and fasting. He has given us the awesome opportunity to talk to Him face-to-face. The veil in the temple has been ripped from top to bottom. We have the power to take America back to God and to goodness in these latter days.

Let's do it! If not now . . . when? If not you . . . who?

Chapter Five

America Under a Curse

For years, preachers have warned from their pulpits that America is heading toward the judgment of God. According to the Bible it is already here, and I am going to show you why that's true and how that judgment is already at work in this country.

With God there are only two choices. Either we live under His blessing or we live under His curse. Incidentally, that choice is ours. God's blessings come from obedience to His Word. His curse comes from disobedience.

The Bible teaches that curses are very real. They can follow a person or a nation for generations, finally breaking them spiritually. Proverbs 26:2 says, "Like a flitting sparrow, like a flying swallow, so a curse without cause shall not alight." When someone speaks a curse against you, and you are not protected by the blood of Christ, that curse will stick. It can follow you and your family for generations.

The "Genesis curse" is an example of a curse that plagues all mankind. When Adam and Eve sinned by partaking of the forbidden fruit, God spoke the curse into existence. God cursed the ground, the woman, the man, the serpent, and Satan. It was a curse that changed mankind forever.

The ground was cursed so that it produced thorns and thistles, weeds and crab grass—and that curse exists to this day. In spite of our ability to attack weeds with powerful chemicals and John Deere tractors, the tares are still with us because of the Genesis curse.

The woman was cursed with the pain of child bearing and monthly menstruation. And she still is.

The man was cursed so that he had to earn his living by the sweat of his brow. And he still has to. All because Adam ate that wretched apple. I'm going to kick his shins the first thing I do when I get to heaven.

The serpent was cursed in that it had to crawl on its belly in the dust from that day forward. When weeds no longer grow, when women no longer have pain in childbirth, when men no longer work to make a living, and when snakes stop crawling . . . the curse will cease. Until then curses are very real!

Christians who believe that such curses cannot be personalized should consider the biblical account of Jacob who unknowingly destroyed his own wife Rachel. Jacob informed his pagan father-in-law, Laban, that he was leaving with Rachel to go to the Promised Land. Unknown to Jacob, Rachel took her father's idols with her. When Laban discovered they were missing, he pursued them, catching up to them in three days.

Laban accused Jacob, saying, "You have stolen my idols!"

Jacob, believing Laban was tricking him to get him to return, spoke a curse: "If any one of my servants has taken your idols, let them die."[1] One year later, his own young wife Rachel died in childbirth.

And that's far from the only illustration of curses in the Bible. Joshua also invoked a curse. After destroying the city of Jericho, Joshua made a bold announcement. "Cursed be the man before the Lord who rises up and builds this city Jericho; he shall lay its foundation with his firstborn, and with his youngest he shall set up its gates."[2] Hundreds of years later, as recorded in I Kings 16:34, a man by the name of Hiel attempted to rebuild the city of Jericho. Just as

Joshua had prophesied, the man's oldest and youngest sons died. Has it happened since? Yes. When I visited Israel a few years ago, the guide told our group that in the 1960s a man tried to rebuild Jericho as a tourist attraction. When he started, his oldest son died instantly and mysteriously. According to the guide, the man immediately stopped work on the cursed city. Had he continued, his youngest son would have also died.[3] I repeat, curses are very real!

Behind every curse is a cause. Anti-Semitism is an example. In Genesis 12:3, God says to Abraham, "I will bless those who bless you, and I will curse him who curses you; and in you all the families of the earth shall be blessed."

It is an historical fact that the nations of the world have been blessed through the Jewish people. Jesus said, "Salvation is of the Jews."[4] The Jewish people gave Christianity the patriarchs—Abraham, Isaac, and Jacob. The Jewish people gave us the prophets—Daniel, Ezekiel, Jeremiah, and Isaiah. There is not a Baptist in the bunch. Contrary to what most renaissance artists depict, Mary, the mother of Jesus, is not an Italian. Mary, Joseph, Jesus, the first family, they are all Jewish. Every word in the Bible was written by Jewish hands. I believe that is why Satan hates the Jewish people so intently. They produced the Word of God, and they produced the Son of God that broke Satan's hold over humanity. I believe that anti-Semitism is a demonic spirit born in the bowels of hell to retaliate against the Jewish people for the good things they have done to bring the light of God to humanity.

It's time for Christians to stop praising the dead Jews of the past, such as Abraham, Issac, and Jacob, while hating the Goldbergs across the street. They are the seed of Abraham, and God loves them. They are the apple of God's eye and they are the family of God. If you bless them, God will bless you. And if you curse them, the judgment of God will come upon you.

The simple fact is, what you do to others, God will do exactly to you. Pharaoh, who drowned the Jewish babies at the time of Moses birth, was later drowned by the hand of God. Haman, who long before Hitler planned the genocide of the Jewish people and built the special gallows to execute the Jewish leader Mordecai, later met his own fate on those very gallows—and so did his family. Exactly what he had intended for the Jewish people happened to him!

The Judgment of God on an Individual

A litany of curses plague individual Americans. A father may place his family under a curse by his dishonest business deals. Proverbs warns: "Whoever rewards evil for good, evil will not depart from his house."[5]

We have seen that curse at work right before our eyes in American history, where several very rich and powerful tycoons made their fortunes illicitly or by grinding the faces of the poor, only to see bizarre accidents cut short the lives of their famous and powerful children. The Bible teaches that such curses follow four generations—160 years. We have seen the troubles spill over to the third generation of some of these great families. Father, if you are making your living by misrepresentation, inside deals, or cheating the public, stop it! You are placing your family under a curse from God. It will stay there for 160 years! Nothing can remove that curse—other than repentance and restitution.

A curse also comes with dishonoring your father and mother. Let me tell you flatly and emphatically that millions of American young people are under this curse of God for their rebellion against their parents. The Bible clearly states that you shall honor your father and your mother "that it may be well with you and you may live long on the earth."[6] Some earthly parents seem to tolerate, even invite, abuse and neglect but your heavenly father is watching, and He is not amused. He will not allow it. Understand this, He will have the last word. He controls your breath and your heartbeat, and He has the muscle to control you.

The Bible teaches that there is a curse on anyone who commits incest. Deuteronomy states, "Cursed is the one who lies with his father's wife."[7] Incest brings God's judgment on an individual. And, because about 25 percent of all American girls are victims of incest, many of America's fathers are under the curse of God. Father, if you are sexually abusing your daughter, you may have your wife intimidated, and you may have your daughter terrorized, but God is not shaking. Don't look back. The judgment of God is right behind you. The only reason He hasn't smashed you like a peanut under the hoof of an elephant is because of His mercy. Do not overstep the bounds of His mercy. God has the power to take you out!

The prophet Zechariah speaks about a curse that afflicts millions of people all over the earth. "Every thief shall be expelled."[8] Do you steal from your employer? God has cut you off. Do you steal from the department store? God has cut you off. When you watch riots unfold on the evening news and you see streams of people hauling merchandise out of stores, remember, God has cut off each and every one of those people. And until these people take it back or make it right, the judgment of God will follow their families for 160 years. If you have stolen, take it back. Make it right.

Perhaps the most common curse on man comes from violating the first commandment: "You shall have no other gods before me." Many people can quote this Scripture but most are unaware of its companion text. Carefully read the words. "You shall not make for yourself any carved image, or any likeness of anything that is heaven above, or that is in the earth beneath, or that is in the water under the earth; you shall not bow down and serve them. For I, the Lord your God, am a jealous God, visiting the iniquity of the fathers on the children to the third and fourth generations of those who hate Me."[9] That's 160 years. God is saying, if you have a statue of any other god in your home, then you hate Me. Jesus said the same thing when He told the disciples, "He who is not with me is against me."[10] You cannot be on both sides of this issue.

The fact is this, false gods empower curses. Statues, crystals, horoscopes, satanism, witchcraft, mind control, and Eastern philosophies are all among the spiritual adulteries that bring the wrath and judgment of God. And, if you put that statue on the dashboard of your car or on your charm bracelet or around your neck, then you are living in what the Bible calls spiritual adultery. And it brings the wrath of God instantly and permanently, until it is repented of and broken in the supernatural. This doesn't just happen sometimes. It happens every time. In their search for truth, the misguided have turned toward evil and they are, by their own hands, falling subject to the curse of God. Sadly, it subjects not only themselves, but their loved ones, the future generations of their family, and their nation as well.

There was a woman in my church years ago who was experiencing a living nightmare. Everything she attempted to achieve would suddenly collapse. She said to me, "I think I'm jinxed. Would you come to my house and see what the Lord would tell you?"

I visited the woman at home one day and saw that the entire inside of the home was filled with statues of dragons. The Bible says that Satan is "that old dragon, the devil." I told her, "Lady, it is my belief that if you recognize Satan in any way, with statues, with the occult, with witchcraft, with mind control, with Eastern philosophies, Satan has a legal right for his demon powers to live in your house. He has a legal right to claim your life, your soul, and your children. And I recommend that you throw them out, and do it now."

She did, and I can tell you that her life turned around immediately and permanently, because she obeyed the Word of God. It is not good enough to recognize God as the first and greatest God. You must recognize Him as the only God. Isaiah 45:21 says, "There is no other God besides Me." Jesus cannot be placed on your mantle among your idols. Jesus is either the Lord of all or He's not Lord at all.

Remember, God plays hardball. He doesn't sit up in Heaven saying, "Oh my goodness, they're not obeying Me." He controls your breath. He controls your heartbeat. God says, "Hey, I can't get his attention." So, He shuts off your business, He sees to it that your new car breaks down once a week, He has your mother-in-law move in with you, He has the IRS call and say, "We'd like to inspect your tax records all the way back to the Civil War."

He puts you in the hospital in a full body cast with your feet and arms suspended in all four directions and you ask, "I wonder if God is trying to speak to me?" Why yes, Bubba, He is.

The Curse on America

As a nation, America is under the curse of God, even now. Look at the Scriptures and decide for yourself. The stand we have taken on abortion, the stand we have taken against God in our classrooms, just may have sealed our doom. Deuteronomy 30:19 says, "I call heaven and earth as witnesses today against you, that I have set before you life and death, blessing and cursing; therefore, choose life, that both you and your descendants may live." Only through God's power and anointing touch can America be saved.

A couple of years ago, *USA Today* printed a front-page picture of five young men, all of them carrying high-powered rifles, pistols, and bullet belts. The accompanying article described how these young men were going to burn down the city of Los Angeles if a high profile court case didn't turn out the way they wanted. City officials were aghast. Newspaper columnists speculated about the social conditions that spawn such violence.

The fact is those young men came from America's public schools where secular humanism has taught them that there is no such thing as right and wrong. It has taught that there are no moral absolutes. It has taught young people to do their own thing. And what is the practical expression of this philosophy? If it feels good, do it. If you want it, steal it. If someone resists you, shoot them.

America's youth are in schools where they get grades that they do not work for from teachers who are afraid to discipline them or simply do not care. This is a blackboard jungle ruled by guns, knives, and fear, an environment of absolute rebellion against authority. Our students are America's new, young barbarians. And this is the generation of the future.

David wrote in Psalm 50:22, "Now consider this, you who forget God, lest I tear you in pieces, and there be none to deliver." I assure you, that stands for America today.

The spirit of this new generation is born in the movie and television studios of Hollywood where macho violence is romanticized, Satan is lord, and witchcraft is the source of power. America's new generation has seen Jesus Christ portrayed as a demonized, lust-driven, spineless buffoon in such movies as *The Last Temptation of Christ*. Hollywood continues to show its hatred towards God, because Hollywood hates Christianity. It is an industry of gluttony, motivated by money and pride, a cancer that eats at the soul of the country.

During the release of *The Last Temptation of Christ*, 25,000 Christians gathered in front of Universal Studios to protest the sacrilege. The movie mongrels of America and their media stooges categorized these Bible-carrying demonstrators as, "the lunatic fringe of religious fanaticism" or "right-wing extremists."

The *Detroit Free Press* called these Christians, "The American ignoramus faction, fun-loathing people full of self-righteous bile."

In contrast, consider how Hollywood and the secular

media responded to concerns by animal rights activists. In 1990, such activists demanded that Disney Studios eliminate a scene from the movie, *White Fang*. They considered the movie to have an anti-wolf theme. The film showed a man being attacked by an unprovoked wolf. Activists claimed that this would never happen, that there was no scientific evidence to support that a wolf would behave in such a way. It is much more popular in America to be anti-Christ, than to be anti-wolf.

In the movie *Cape Fear*, a vicious rapist-murder is portrayed as a Pentecostal Christian. He has tattoos of the cross on his body and Scripture verses on his arm. As he rapes his victims, he asks them, "Are you ready to be born again and speak in tongues?" What do you think would happen if any other minority group in America was so reviled and miscast? The makers of such a movie would be swimming in lawsuits and making mountains of apologies and settlements. Christianity bashing, however, is considered an art form in Hollywood.

Christianity and morality are not only losing in the movie theaters, the same theme is now running through American popular music. The young gangsters who have taken over America's streets use violent rap music for their inspiration. Time-Warner produced the hit song "Cop Killer," which encouraged a New York youth to murder a policeman in cold blood. Rock music, in general, often promotes drug abuse, satanism, rape, murder, and suicide.

In his insightful book, *Cults That Kill*, Larry Kahaner tells the story of a sixteen-year-old boy who attended a rock concert, received a message from Satan, and took an oath to carry it out. When he returned home, he murdered his father and mother, and with their blood, wrote "Hail Satan" on the wall.[11] This is today's America. "The wicked shall be be turned into hell, / And all the nations that forget God."[12]

Murders have now surpassed automobile accidents as the number one cause of death among young blacks. The majority of these murders are black-on-black. Most of these new killers are the products of fatherless homes. Twenty-five percent of America's adult black male population is in prison or on parole. And of all the fathers, both black and white who are present in their homes, they will average only forty-five seconds a day talking with their children.[13]

Many parents who don't have time for their children simply place them in front of the television set. The average child will spend more than forty-eight hours a week watching television. It has become the great baby-sitter, teacher, and brainwasher. The outcome is a generation filled with violence, lust, greed, witchcraft, and fear. Meanwhile, American parents ignorantly sit by and let strangers teach and control their children, every single day, through the medium of television. The time has come for Christian parents to become the stewards and the watchdogs of their children. If a television program does not glorify God and the purity of His holiness, turn it off. At least for now, we have that much power over our enemies.

The Curse on the Home

In the remarkable twenty-eighth chapter of Deuteronomy, Moses outlines the curses God will place on a people or nation that is disobedient to Him. It is a frightening litany of evil that begins in the home, moves to the city, and eventually affects the economy of a whole nation.

First, Moses warns, "You shall betroth a wife, but another man will lie with her; you shall build a house, but you shall not dwell in it." This speaks of the destruction of the traditional family. "Another man shall lie with her" speaks of rampant adultery followed by divorce. Children are scarred and scattered like straw in a tornado.

The future of America is not going to be determined by politicians in Washington, D.C., but by godly parents teaching their children the precepts of the Word of God. Our children must know the teachings of righteousness, truth, and integrity before they can apply these principles to their lives and country. This is the foundation upon which America can stand.

Second, in describing God's curse against a disobedient people, Moses warns, "Your sons and your daughters shall be given to another people, and your eyes shall look and fail with longing for them all day long."

Does America enjoy her children? With few exceptions, the answer is no. Four thousand of them are murdered every day in America's abortion mills. *Home Alone* is not just a movie, it is a subconscious parody of a national tragedy. Child abuse is a national shame. Vile, tear-jerking, child pornography is a vicious, multibillion dollar industry in our country. Meanwhile, nude pictures of children in various adult poses are subsidized by grants offered by our government and labeled by the media as "art." Your tax dollars at work!

Do we enjoy our children? Ask the thousands of missing children whose faces appear on milk cartons that question. It seems that if a child escapes the abortionist's knife, a host of other evils are anxiously awaiting: drug pushers, molesters, satanists, homosexuals, feminists. Even our government awaits their arrival as they dictate the humanistic teachings in our schools. Forty years ago people did not believe in a real devil. Today, hundreds of thousands openly worship Satan, murdering children in the sacrificial honor of his name. Do we love our children? I think the answer is clear. We will explore the curse on the home more fully in Chapter 6, "Witchcraft in Your House!"

Third, in describing God's curse against a disobedient people, Moses declared, "Cursed shall you be in the city."

The Curses of the Cities

Take a good look at the cities of America. Riot-stricken Los Angeles is a time bomb waiting to explode. Gangs rule the inner city. New York's boroughs are still controlled by organized crime, either the mafia or the new Chinese syndicates. San Francisco is governed by homosexuals. Las Vegas is controlled by the lords of casinos. And, in New Orleans, prostitution rackets have taken over the city. America's cities are suffering under the load of lawlessness. The jails are flooded with criminals. Murderers and rapists roam free from early paroles. You know that justice has been turned upside-down when a mugger can hit you in the head with a pipe and be out of jail before you are out of the hospital.

We sing about an America that is "the land of the free and the home of the brave"; meanwhile, we live behind locked doors and barred windows. Our homes are equipped with state-of-the-art burglar alarm systems. Attack dogs are straining at the leashes. Ladies carry mace on their key chains. Doors have multiple locks. Guns are cocked and loaded. Burglar bars are over our windows. We, the tax-paying citizens of America, are prisoners in our own homes and victims on our own streets. It you think America is free, you are deceived.

Fourth, Moses warns, "Cursed shall be your basket and your kneading bowl." He is, of course, referring to the economy.

The Economic Curse

And exactly how is America's economy doing?

- The United States of America is nearly $5 trillion in debt, and that debt continues to race out of sight at a rate of about $1 billion a day.
- Just to pay the interest, the national debt needs all of the taxes collected from every citizen west of the Mississippi.
- The federal debt currently stands close to $18,000 for every man, woman, and child in America.

- One leading economist has warned that, "we are racing towards a bankruptcy that will place our children and our grandchildren in an economic slavery to foreign countries. America is blindly moving towards becoming a third-world economy, and there will be no recovery simply because we have spent beyond our means for forty years."[14]

- In the insightful book *Banking on the Brink*, one leading economist has predicted that more than two thousand banks in America will soon take a dive.[15] Banks don't fail, they merge. Notice how we now have more megabanks and fewer smaller ones? This means there is more wealth in the hands of fewer people, which was a major cause of the crash of 1929.

- The savings and loan crashes will eventually cost the coming generation $1.3 trillion plus interest.

- A pension crisis is now hanging over the heads of American workers, the result of greedy, get-rich-quick, junk-bond investments in the market. Most of it is paper and now worthless.

Just on the horizon is the greatest economic crisis we have faced since independence. For years, the federal government has been raiding the social security fund. They have taken billions of dollars from this trust, replacing it with IOUs worth only what the government is willing and able to pay. In the past decade, that great resource has been bled dry and no one knows how to put it back in order. One so-called "solution" is to extend the retirement age to seventy and pocket the money that should go to retirees. Another is to demand a forfeit of benefits to all who are entitled to social security, but have enough money to live on. The government, of course, will decide what constitutes enough.

The result is the richest country in the world now faces an uncertain financial future simply because our government couldn't control its own spending. During the Reagan administration the Grace Commission conducted an in-depth study to show how America spends its money. It found that for every dollar in new taxes, the government spends $1.80.

The economic options for America are few. Someday in the near future, an American president will be faced with just two choices: Either he will declare America bankrupt, or he will instruct the Treasury Department to print more money, launching a round of hyper-inflation that will destroy our economy.

Fifth, in describing God's curse against a disobedient nation, Moses warns, "The Lord will make the plague cling to you until He has consumed you."

The Curse of the Plagues

AIDS is one such incurable plague. No matter what new medical breakthroughs come forth, AIDS is still as deadly as ever. Everyone who contracts AIDS dies. And the fact is, there are tens-of-thousands of silent carriers of the disease in America.

But there is good news. Every born-again believer who has been washed in the blood of Jesus Christ has a life insurance policy that no one can take away. Psalm 91:10 states, "No evil shall befall you, nor shall any plague come near your dwelling." There is hope. AIDS is no match for the power of Almighty God.

Just as huge portions of the population have succumbed to AIDS, many more have died on the battlefields fighting for America. Examine what Moses said in Deuteronomy 28:25, "The Lord will cause you to be defeated before your enemies; you shall go out one way against them and flee seven ways before them." God judges and destroys a nation for its sin. Israel lost the battle at Ai because of the sin of one its sons. In our lifetime we have seen weak enemies, without international diplomatic clout, without great financial resources, without advanced weapons, defeat America. We lost in Korea. We lost in Vietnam.

Victory even eluded America in Desert Storm. Even after the triumphant destruction of our enemy with overwhelming weapons and overwhelming odds, he has crawled right out from underneath a rock to snub us again. What changed with the billions of dollars spent on Desert Storm? Sadaam Hussein is still in power. He still works toward nuclear capability. He still threatens Israel. He still intends to conquer Jerusalem. And the people we went to help, the Kuwaitis, see us as such an unreliable partner they are limiting our ground troops in their country lest they provoke Hussein.

Sixth, Moses warns the disobedient nation that, "the alien who is among you shall rise higher and higher above you, and you shall come down lower and lower." Hosea wrote, "Aliens have devoured his strength, but he does not know it."[16]

The Curse of Servitude

Foreign countries are currently buying our land, businesses, real estate, and industry out from under our feet. The foreigners are not to blame, but whose financial interest do you think they are going to protect? Our national leaders tell us that economic time bombs have been planted on Wall Street. Other nations have so much interest in stocks and bonds, they hold America hostage. If Congress does not vote the way they want, they threaten to pull out. The result could be disastrous. Our economy would literally plunge and collapse overnight. We are not in control of America's economic destiny. Other countries are.

Solutions do not rest with our Congress or national leaders; they rest solely with the Church of Jesus Christ. The Bible tells us in 2 Chronicles 7:14, "If My people who are called by My name will humble themselves, and pray and seek My face, and turn from their wicked ways, then I will hear from heaven, and will forgive their sin and heal their land." This is our call to return to absolute loyalty to the Word of God. It is our only hope to take our country out of the hands of the foreign powers holding us hostage.

In our calling to absolute loyalty to God, we must, as a nation, stand up for that which is right and clearly oppose the wrong. Remember, God is watching. He is the only one to fear.

When the president stands before the nation and calls for homosexuals to be legally acknowledged by allowing them into the military, we as a nation must rise up and let him hear our voices: "No! While we have great love for every single human being, that behavior is an abomination under the Word of God. We will not accept it!"

When Hillary Clinton calls for the children to have the right to sue their parents for divorce, we must let her hear our voices: "No! Children, honor your father and your mother, that your days may be long upon the earth."

If the welfare department continues to tax men who work, and then give money to men who can work but will not work, we must take a stand against it and let the nation's leaders hear our voices: "No! The man who does not work will not eat."

We must make the Word of God known to our children, known to our neighbors, and known to our politicians; it is our only hope. If we are ridiculed and demeaned, so what? Jesus was ridiculed and demeaned. If we are outlawed and imprisoned, so what? David was an outlaw. Peter and Paul were both imprisoned.

Remember, the basis of either a blessing or a curse is obedience to God's Word. Has America been obedient? The answer is obvious. America's number one problem is not the economy, it is not the crime rate, it is not our corrupt politicians. America's number one problem is the judgment of God, because God hates sin and America is saturated with it.

The solution is not in the hands of our politicians, our Congress, our government. The only solution is in the hands of every believing Christian who has the faith to pray and believe that once again God will bless America and raise her up as a testimony to the world. God is the only one who can save us. In Genesis, he scooped up a handful of dirt, and he breathed into it and man became a living soul. The God that we serve is the Creator, our Lord, and our Master. He is the only God, and He is our only salvation.

PART TWO

Deception in the Home

Chapter Six

Witchcraft in Your House

Deception in government and public life cannot hold a candle to the witchcraft that has invaded the homes of America in these latter days. Divorce is now epidemic and seen as a cure-all to any marital conflict. Some new state laws make it easier to get a divorce than a driver's license. Feminists are trying to tell us that there is little difference between the sexes. Fashion designers encourage boys to carry purses and girls to carry footballs. Biblical teaching about marriage and the home, which has been an essential part of Western civilization since Constantine, has been unceremoniously dropped.

The spin-off has been catastrophic. America is engulfed in a tidal wave of venereal disease, juvenile crime, and a new category of poverty: single family homes. For the last thirty years, America has been in a moral free fall.

Here is the irony. While screamers in Hollywood complain that Christian political activists are trying to ram their theology down the throats of society by legislating morality, they, themselves, have rammed their godless philosophy down the throats of American youth. Seeking to justify their own perverse lifestyle, the entertainment industry has glamorized and promoted the downfall of the American marriage. In motion pictures and television sitcoms promiscuity and sex outside of marriage are romanticized with only token acknowledgment to the pain and consequences. Venereal disease is given a new designer name, STD, socially transmitted disease. One young teenager said, "I think herpes is sexy." So rampant is America's abandonment of the monogamous relationship that new strains of incurable genital warts have started appearing.

I've got news for you. Divorce is not the solution. Sociologist Lenore Whitesman states that the average woman's standard of living will decline 73 percent within the first year of her divorce. Contrary to what you've seen from Hollywood, it is not a passport to paradise. It is a ticket to a living hell. The survival rate of second marriages is a mere 30 percent. The survival rate of a third marriage is 15 percent, and it goes downhill from there.

Diane Medved, author of *The Case Against Divorce,* offers clear and convincing evidence that the aftereffects of divorce are almost always worse than the original problem. Former marriage partners and children are often damaged physically as well as emotionally. The pain lingers for years. Most counselors have learned that the initial, conscious level of pain will last at least half the time of the relationship, which means that the breakup of a twenty-year marriage will require at least ten years to heal. But even then, some scars will linger.[1]

Make no mistake about it, your marriage, your children, and family life in America are under attack in these latter days. Values and principles that have guided civilized man for centuries are coming unraveled by the minute. You can't hide from it. You can't wish it away. And you certainly can't afford to be lulled into a catatonic, self-deceived state of ignorance. Survival is dependent on knowing and understanding the events swirling around you and then acting according to the emergency plan laid out in Scripture.

The American Family

What is a family? The word has been used by so many groups to mean so many things that it has lost the essence of its meaning. In the movie *The Godfather*, Vito Corleone describes his band of cold-blooded Mafia murderers as "family." When Charles Manson was on his murdering spree through southern California, leaving the blood of movie stars splattered on the walls with gory graffiti, he called the mindless group of riffraff who followed him his "family." The Atlanta Braves call themselves a "family." In churches across the world we sing songs about "the family of God."

Today, social revisionists in America are trying to redefine the word *family* to mean "two consenting adults and their children." There is a massive lobby with millions of dollars behind it. The reason? So homosexuals can live together, adopt children, earn same-sex benefits, and be socially acceptable. With superior earning power and no family to support, they can form political action committees, pass laws, and control government. They can throw preachers in jail for preaching the Word of God, but they are still not a family and never will be a family according to God's Word.

A family is not a house with a prestigious address. A roof will keep out the rain. Four walls will keep out the cold night wind. A floor will support the tottering steps of the infant or the aged. A door will welcome friends and keep out enemies. A fireplace will warm those who nestle close on a cold winter's night, but this is not a family.

A family is the picture of a mother cooking dinner for people she loves. A family is the laugh of a baby. It is the strength of the presence of the father. A family is the loving warmth of hearts, light from happy eyes, kindness, loyalty, and covenant love and demonstration. A family home should be the first school and the first church that a child ever attends. It is there that a child should learn to pray. It is there that a child should see from the father how to treat the mother. It is there a child should see from the mother how women relate to men. It is there, long before school begins, that a child should learn from its parents what is right and what is wrong.

Families are where you go for comfort when you are hungry or sick or when you have been battered and bruised by the world. Families open the very doors of heaven and heal you. They anoint your wounds with the oil of gladness and wrap their loving arms about you.

Families are where joy is shared. They will be delighted with your promotion on the job. They will be proud of you for making the honor roll in the public school. They will buy every newspaper on the rack when your name is in it as the high school football hero, debate star, cheerleader, or valedictorian.

Families are where children respect fathers and mothers. They're never called "old man" or "old lady." In advancing years, they're not shuffled to the sidelines to be ignored. Whether they are in a wheelchair or reclining on a couch too feeble to sit erectly, they are there because they belong.

Families are where children are considered the blessings of the Lord and not looked upon as an inconvenience to a precious career. They're not considered detestable because they might destroy the high-school figure of the mother. They are angels unaware that God has sent into the care of a husband and wife for a very few days until they go into society to make their own contributions. Families are where the simplest food is good enough for kings because it has been earned with the sweat of an honest day's labor. That's family, and may God bless it and preserve it in these United States of America. Yet what occurred in the beginning, still occurs now.

What Occurred in the Beginning, Still Occurs

Genesis is called the book of beginnings. Everything God wanted to begin began in Genesis. The plan of salvation itself begins in Genesis. Satan also began his plan to destroy your home in Genesis. The book begins with a crisis between man and woman.

- In Genesis 1, the heavens and earth were created by the spoken Word of Almighty God.
- In Genesis 3, man rebelled against God's spoken Word. Satan deceived Adam and Eve, saying "Has God indeed said . . . ?"
- In Genesis 4, there is murder as Cain killed Abel.
- In Genesis 9, there is pornography.
- In Genesis 15, God gave Abraham a blood covenant for the Promised Land.
- In Genesis 16 there is adultery.
- In Genesis 19, there is homosexuality.
- In Genesis 34, there is fornication.
- In Genesis 38, there is incest and prostitution.
- In Genesis 39, there is the seduction of Joseph by Potiphar's wife.

Why is there such a conflict in the American home? Because Satan has been busy laying his plan to destroy you. Now, thousands of years after the experiences of Genesis, you go home, turn on the television, and the very same temptations come into your living room. There is the theme of man versus woman, of polygamy and pornography. There is adultery, fornication, homosexuality, incest, prostitution, and seduction. And you sit there and suck it all in. Dad, do you think that some lines written by Norman Lear, a man who is single-handedly trying to bring down family values in America, are going to edify your children? Mom, when you hear some television star rail against her husband with the most vindictive and vicious words imaginable, do you think that you are influenced?

You say, "Not me. I can censor all those thing in my mind. I know what I believe."

Let me tell you something. Big business doesn't pay a million dollars a minute to advertise if it doesn't have influence. Everything you and your family sees goes right into your little Univac. Click. It's in there. Jesus says that "out of the abundance of the heart man speaks."[2] How many abundant hours of television are in your sub-conscious? Compare it to the number of hours you spend reading the Bible with your family. Who is Lord of your home: the Holy Spirit or Hollywood?

The reason most American homes are breaking apart is because we have allowed our intellect, our emotions, and our spirits to be pickled and duped by a secular society that is doing nothing more than taking the seduction plan of Genesis, putting it into a Hollywood script, and pouring it out for America.

This book is a warning. It is Satan's desire to destroy your family, your marriage, and your children. If you can't see it, then you are deceived. It is God's desire that you be in health and prosper, spiritually and materially, and that you be filled with His Spirit. I'm saying to you in Jesus name, generally the best thing on secular television is the knob that turns it off.

Instead turn on the Word of God and be filled with the Spirit. Drink in Living Water, not Hollywood's toxic waste.

And God Created Woman

The American church has done a disservice to the women of this nation because it has failed to portray the successful woman as a mother. Nothing on this earth is more honorable than being a godly mother. Though the press and the media applaud women who become bankers or judges or politicians, God's Word paints the portrait of a mother as the ultimate success story. Nothing is more praiseworthy. Nothing is more holy. Nothing is more lofty. God did not say to Eve, "Go forth and become the CEO of General Motors." He told man to work. He told the woman to "go forth, be fruitful and multiply." God's top priority for you is to be a mother. That's a command.

CEO of the Home

A mother is a chauffeur, a chef, a social director, a banker, a boss, and a zookeeper. In motherhood, a woman is fulfilling one of her God-given reasons for existence.

God's command is to be fruitful and multiply.[3] When you reject God's plan, you reject truth. And when you reject truth, all that is left is a lie. God's Word is very clear; if you obey the Lord, you prosper. If you rebel against God, the judgment of God comes against you. I am telling you, the judgment of God is not coming to America; the judgment of God is on America right now. And it is manifest in this single command: Be fruitful and multiply.

I hear ladies saying, "Well, I'd like to have a baby but you know this is a very troubled time to bring a new child into the world." When Moses was born, the government was drowning all Jewish male babies in the Nile River. When Jesus Christ was born, King Herod was sending out his elite palace guard to butcher every child within a ten-mile radius of his birthplace. For a sinful world in rebellion against God, it is always a dangerous and troubled time to give birth to an innocent and vulnerable child. Quit worrying about Washington's policies and start thinking about God's policies. Live according to God's policies and so shall you "prosper and be in health."

Motherhood

What does God expect from the mother? Proverbs 31 paints the portrait.

She is virtuous. Proverbs asks, "Who can find a virtuous woman, for her price is far above rubies?" Ladies, teenage daughter, your virtue makes you priceless. Teenage girl, if you're dating some hormone hurricane who has the urge to merge, and he says something stupid like, "Honey, to prove your love to me, let's go all the way," you slap his face until his ears ring like chapel bells on a cold Christmas morning. Then get out of his car and take a cab home.

There's a difference between love and lust, and many don't know the difference, so let me give you three quick lessons:

1. Love gives. Lust takes.
2. Love gives a ring. Lust gives a condom.
3. Love is patient, kind, and understanding. Lust is rude, crude, and very demanding.

You ought to write that down somewhere until you can say it in your sleep.

She provides food. "She rises while it is yet night, and gives food to her household." She knows how to make something for supper other than reservations.

She is a worker. "Her candle does not go out by night." She gets up early. She stays up late. She's not sitting on a couch eating bonbons watching Sally Jesse Raphael.

She is discrete. "In her mouth is the law of kindness." She's not some party girl from an Ivy League school who can outcuss a Marine drill sergeant. Some people make you glad when they come. Other people make you glad when they go. You're always glad to meet the woman of Proverbs 31. She is married and a mother, in that order, something America's young people need to get in their minds.

She is submitted to her own husband. It's taught in the Old Testament. It's taught in the New Testament. It's taught by Paul. It's taught by Peter. It isn't popular, but it is everywhere in the Bible—that submission thing.

That Submission Thing

Compare those famous verses in Ephesians 5:22–24 to what the Bible says in Colossians 3:18. "Wives submit to your own husbands, as is fitting in the Lord." Look at the Bible record of trouble that started when a man submitted to the lead of his wife. Not to the *need* of his wife, but to the *lead* of his wife.

Adam listened to Eve, and God kicked them out of the Garden of Eden because he ate the forbidden fruit. It was God's intention for his human creation to enjoy the pleasures of the Garden of Eden. And no mosquitoes. But Adam took the fruit, and between the two of them they ate us out of house and home.

I came home one day after work and Diane was fixing dinner in the kitchen; so I just stood by talking about my day. "Here," she said and she brought some food up to my mouth. "Eat this." Like some obedient beast, I ate it. "Now," she said, "see how easy that was?" All right, but I'm still going to kick Adam in the shins when I get to heaven.

Abraham also listened to his wife, Sarah. They had been trying to have children for years but Sarah was barren, so she said, "Go to my maid, Hagar, and have a baby with her."

Abraham said, "Sounds like the will of God to me." Zip . . . off to Hagar's tent. Not long after Hagar was pregnant, Sarah relaxed and became pregnant herself. Now she and Abraham were finally going to have a child of their own. Dreams do come true. But when Sarah's and Hagar's boys were born, Sarah changed her mind. She decided that Hagar and her son Ishmael should go and that Abraham should be the one to kick them out. Abraham obeyed. Hagar and her son, Abraham's own firstborn, were ordered out into the wilderness.

Hagar almost died but God was watching and always protects the innocent. The problem is, that little boy Ishmael grew up to be the father of the Arabs. Sarah's baby was Isaac, the father of the Jews. What started out as a family feud six thousand years ago is now an international crisis in the Middle East. It happened because a man listened to his wife's command—not God's!

Women's liberation is not about equal pay for equal work. Women's liberation is about authority. It's about who is going to lead in the home and who is going to lead in the workplace. The greatest battle in the American home is the battle for authority. Who is the head of the house? One body with two heads is a freak. One family with two heads is a war zone.

Righteous authority is given by God to men to lovingly lead the home and for kings and all who are in authority to rule in government. God says, "I have given that righteous authority to Adam. It is his. He is the head of the house." Anyone who attacks the husband's authority is literally attacking God's plan. God operates through delegated authority, which is a righteous authority. In the home, God operates through the authority of the father. In the nation, He operates through governments, as outlined in the eighth chapter of Romans.

Unrighteous authority is given by Satan to rebel against God's plan for man. Everything Satan does is through unrighteous authority, and it is diametrically opposed to God's rule. Witchcraft is the method used to carry out Satan's unrighteous authority. The three manifestations of witchcraft are manipulation, intimidation, and domination.

Let me give you an example. The little lady of the house lets the man know that if he will do what she wants him to do, or if he will buy what she wants him to buy, the bedroom will come alive tonight. But if he doesn't, it will be as cold as an iceberg.

That's witchcraft, pure and simple. The Bible says, "The wife does not have authority over her own body, but the husband does . . ."[4]

Women who control their house with bad moods are practicing witchcraft. Jezebel controlled Israel by manipulating Ahab through her moods. The Bible says there was never a woman on the face of the earth like Jezebel. I have heard husbands say, "I have to give in to my wife or she'll be angry for days." I want you to understand something.

When you give into that, you only feed it. It grows. It multiplies. You are not doing your wife a favor. In the long run you are only going to make her miserable. She is exhibiting a spirit of witchcraft, and if it works, she'll keep using it to dominate you. Stand up. You are the head of that house. Get out from under the bed and take charge.

Guilt is also the chief weapon of the manipulator. The wife says to the husband, "I just want to remind you that I almost died giving birth to your son." Of course, the husband is now sixty-two years old but she wants to remind him of that pain. "I married you when my mother said I shouldn't, bless her sacred memory. And ten years ago, you were late for supper, and don't you forget it." That is manipulation through guilt. That's witchcraft.

How do you break that cycle? It is not by evasion; witchcraft seeks to control without confrontation. The Bible says to confront, "speaking the truth in love."[5] So, when you have a problem with your spouse, don't run away; look at the problem, eyeball to eyeball, and lovingly with spiritual principles, resolve it.

Some wives will complain, "But I can't trust my husband's leadership. He doesn't make good decisions." He decided to marry you, didn't he?

Women and the Church

The Bible says in 1 Timothy 2:9 that "woman adorn themselves in modest apparel." What you wear says a lot about you. There have been books written on the subject. I have a psychology text in my office that says bizarre dress is a sign of being mentally disturbed. If that's true, half of America must be having a nervous breakdown!

Wife, according to the Word of God, your dress is to be modest. If you want people to treat you maturely as a human being with sensitivities, dreams, and hopes like anybody else, then dress like it. Modest apparel is more than good taste, it shows that you have some self-respect.

Likewise, in his letter to Timothy, Paul says that a

woman should not be a showcase for her husband's wealth. She should not be a walking boutique of gold, pearls, and designer dresses. God is not crass. He has good taste. And He is not nouveau riche. His wealth has been around for years. He wants to be proud of us, so He cares enough to teach us what to wear.

Paul's letter is very clear. The woman is not to have spiritual authority over a man. A pastor is someone with spiritual authority. To ordain a woman as a pastor over a man violates the very clear teaching of the apostle Paul. Ordaining women is not progress, it is contrary to the teaching and the preaching of God's Word. Yes, the lady can have a healing ministry. Yes, the lady can have a teaching ministry. Yes, the lady can work under her husband's authority. But she is not to be the pastor of the church. That is the teaching of the Word of God.

But why so strict? Why does Paul say that women must even be "silent in the church?"

In an orthodox synagogue, the men and women were separated. When Paul or anyone else was teaching, an aggressive woman would call over to her husband, "Hey Abe, what's he saying? Do you agree with that?"

Paul said, "Talk it over at home. I don't want the whole church service torn up by a family discussion."

In 1 Timothy the Bible gives clear instructions for widows. The Bible says that widows are to be honored, to be cared for, to be supported. But the Bible has some clear qualifiers. The widow must be sixty years of age. She must have been faithful to her husband. She must have trained her children well. She must have shown hospitality to the saints, helping those in trouble and devoting her life to good deeds. That's what constitutes a biblical widow. Somebody who lived her life down at the Crystal Pistol and now comes walking down the aisle to get saved and says, "Take care of me," is not a biblical widow. That's not how it works. You invest your life in the kingdom of God, and then the kingdom of God takes care of you. That's how it works.

There's more. If a widow has children or grandchildren, those children should support her. Remember, the Bible says that anyone who does not provide for his own has abandoned the faith and is worse than an unbeliever.[6] It does not apply exclusively to men.

Chapters two and three of the book of Titus say that older women are to teach younger women "how to be sober, how to love their husbands, how to love their children, and how to be keepers of the home." Is that what young people are being taught in Christian homes today? No. Generally, the older women in the American home are saying, "Honey, if old meathead opens his mouth, you tell him, 'It's my way or the highway. Hit it.'"

We have a new generation of parents who were raised without discipline. They got anything they wanted when they wanted it. And when they got married and had to work with a marriage partner instead of pliable old Mom and Pop, they were shocked.

Do you know why the McDonald's Company is hiring older people right now? Because they know how to work. There is a generation of young people who don't know how to do anything but toast pop tarts and push buttons on television remote controls. And the generation right behind them is in worse trouble. Social workers can tell you who is raising the children of America today. Either the jailhouse, a day care, or grandparents. At least the grandparents know how to take care of children. This "me first" generation doesn't know. It wasn't taught.

Children of today can say, "If I want it, give it to me now. If you don't, I'll throw a fit and embarrass you. If you spank me in public, you can get arrested."

I want you to understand that when you accept God's portrait of the family that nonsense stops. The father leads, the wife submits to that lead, and their children honor them as the authority in their lives . . . and if they don't their backside burns.

In the past thirty years, the parents of America have

relinquished their children and turned them over to the state. I want to tell you something. There's not a verse in the Book that says your children belong to the state of Texas, or your children belong to Washington, D.C. Mother, the children in your house were given to you by God, Himself. They are your children, and you need to act like it and you need to fight for their spiritual survival.

The Word of God is calling for pure, chaste, honorable women who love their children, care for their parents, and show hospitality to all. That's the portrait of God's perfect woman. And that's as far away from the stereotypical "babe" in the cigarette commercials as it is from "the church lady" on *Saturday Night Live*.

Chapter Seven

Dads of Deception

Before God was a judge, He was a Father. Before He was a creator, He was a Father, and as a Father, He has established the biblical pattern of family government. He understands our psychological needs. He knows all about our desires, and He has taken the time to tell us what He expects from each member of the family.

In the Word of God, the father is provider, priest, prophet, and king. As provider, he works. As priest, he guides. As prophet, he protects. And as king, he governs.

The Man as Provider

The Bible's caution, "If any provide not for his own . . . he hath denied the faith and is worse than an infidel,"[1] applies especially to the head of the house, the father. These are powerful words, and America needs to hear them. While the rest of the world has abandoned their experimentation with socialism and declared it dead, we are being led by a brainless cadre of wealthy media elitists who want to salve their guilty consciences by forcing it down our throats. The media tell us that the government has a responsibility to bail us out. But God expects dads to get up and go to work and provide for their families. If you are physically ill or handicapped and can't work, that's another story. If you are physically able, and don't work, you are worse than an infidel in the eyes of God.

You say, "Well, doesn't God provide?" Yes, He does. He provides worms for the birds, but he doesn't throw them down their throats. You get up and go get it. As long as you do your part, God will do His part. Every miracle has two parts: your part and God's part. The old saying "Work like everything depends on you, pray like everything depends on God" is all too true. Remember the Bible says, "If anyone will not work, neither shall he eat."[2]

God, Himself, is a provider. He is *Jehovah-Jireh*, and He expects earthly fathers to provide for their own. America is now saturated with a growing subculture called "deadbeat dads": men who sire children with their live-in lover or wife-of-the-week and then leave them stranded and alone to care for the baby. That is not sexual independence; it is moral insanity. Citizens of America, we need to send a very clear message to these deadbeat dads, "Provide for the needs of that mother and that child, or go to jail and stay there."

Hollywood public relations people fawn over movie stars who raise and support illegitimate children. Meanwhile, the father is off in another relationship in search of himself. The television sitcom, *Murphy Brown,* tried to cloak the whole experience with respectability. Madonna gave birth out-of-wedlock and Hollywood applauded. But it isn't a laughing matter to a sixteen-year-old girl in the projects whose life is ruined, who can't support herself or her baby, and who is now headed for generations of welfare dependence. Sexual freedom is not the right to do as you please. Freedom is the right to do as you ought, and the Bible, God's instruction manual, will show the way. Winston Churchill said, "Responsibility is the price of greatness."

God the Father is also *Jehovah Shammah*, which simply means, "The Lord is there." Make no mistake about it, God expects the earthly father "to be there." Many fathers are gone. They simply abandon the home. Some are gone even when they're home. They are more committed to their work and their career than to their wife and children. Some provide rooms full of toys and yards full of plastic playhouses and cars, but provide no emotional, spiritual, or intellectual support. In that sense, they are gone.

Sociologists now have a name for these people. They are called "phantom fathers." Where are they? One study showed that, "69 percent of rapists, 72 percent of adolescent murderers, and 70 percent of long-term prison inmates, once lived in a fatherless home."[3]

Forty percent of America's children now live in homes without their biological father. By the year 2000, our government says, 60 percent of all children born in the United States will be illegitimate. We are watching the death and destruction of America.

What does God think about it? Malachi 4:6 says, "And he will turn the hearts of the fathers to the children . . . Lest I come and strike the earth with a curse." Have you ever had a father or a mother who took that seriously? Mine did.

Bill Bennett, former secretary of education and drug czar, marshaled the data on what has happened to the fatherless American home during past thirty years. Those stats? A 560 percent increase in violent crime; a 400 percent increase in juvenile arrests; a 200 percent increase in teenage suicide.[4] All this while the American people were spending billions of dollars to conquer the problem.

I said in Chapter 5 that America's major problem is not poverty, crime, or the government. America's number one problem is the judgment of God, and God is judging this country for fathers missing from the home. We need a program to get him back in the house to raise the children he's fathered. God has that program.

The Man As Priest of His Family

As priest, the father represents his family to God. In Exodus you will read the story of the Passover. In spite of

127

a series of plagues that ravaged the land, the stubborn government of Pharaoh would not release the Israelite slaves. So God sent his death angel to pass over the city. The angel would take the firstborn son of every Egyptian family. Each Israelite family was warned to sacrifice a lamb and sprinkle its blood over the doorposts. This was the father's responsibility.[5] Without that blood, the family would be visited with death. The safety of the family depended on what each father did. If the father failed, the oldest son died.

In our generation, the death angel is passing over the United States of America, and he's coming with drugs and sexual disease and rebellion. Dad, if you don't take the blood of the cross and place it over the doors of your soul and the souls of your children, your family doesn't have a chance of survival.

In the first chapter of Job, the father offered a burnt sacrifice for each son and each daughter by name to protect them from the judgment of God. He knew that if he failed to do that, if he failed to represent his children to God by name, his children would be destroyed. Dad, do you represent your children to God? If not you, who? And if not now, when are you going to do it? America's children are being destroyed by fathers who refuse to be the priest of their homes.

The priest leads his family in worship. I am not concerned about the schoolhouse nearly as much as I am concerned about your house, because it's not the schoolteacher's responsibility to teach your child to pray, and it's not the schoolteacher's responsibility to teach your child the principles of God's Word. It's your responsibility.

Let me tell you a little secret learned from years of marriage counseling. Prayer produces intimacy, and with spiritual intimacy, there can be truly fulfilling sexual intimacy. Marriage is spiritual and nothing accentuates the intimacy of your marriage more than prayer.

When Moses went to Mount Sinai, it was the place of prayer. He stayed so long that the Bible says, "God spoke to him face-to-face, as a man speaks to his friend."[6] In other words, God, Himself, became intimate through prayer. On the day of Pentecost, the disciples prayed until they were in one accord. They became so intimate in that ten days of prayer, they went out and sold everything they had to help one another. When you pass the offering plate in the average church today, you're lucky to get the plates back!

The Man As Prophet in His Home

As a priest, man represents the family to God, as a prophet he reverses the flow. Man, the prophet, represents God to his family.

The Bible says in Genesis 6:8 that "Noah found grace in the eyes of the Lord." And the Lord said to Noah, "Come into the ark, you and all your household . . ."[7] God spoke to Noah, the father, and told him what to do. God described the coming flood. He told the father how to escape, and in the end "Only Noah and those who were with him in the ark remained alive."

Hebrews 11:7 says, "By faith, Noah, being divinely warned of things not yet seen, moved with godly fear, prepared an ark for the saving of his household." Hear me, Dad. There will come a time in America when your family will be saved depending on what you hear from God. There will come a time in the life of your family when they will live or die spiritually based on what you hear from God. You are the priest and you are the prophet.

As Prophet the Father Is on Guard.

The Bible says Satan is going about like a roaring lion seeking to devour, and he seeks to devour your family. He seeks to devour your wife and your children. You guard them by teaching them the Word of God. Satan is not impressed by the peppy, motivational slogans that you bring home from the chamber of commerce. He's not diminished by the Boy Scouts or the Girl Scouts or the Little League, but the devil is destroyed by the Word of God. He knows its power.

In one parable, Jesus described a rich man and a beggar named Lazarus. The rich man died and went to hell. Lazarus died and was "carried to the bosom of Abraham." From hell the rich man called out to Abraham to send Lazarus to talk to his family still on earth. But Abraham rebuked him, saying, "If they don't hear Moses and the prophets, neither will they be persuaded [to repent] . . ."[8]

The Psalmist says, "Your word have I hidden in my heart, / That I might not sin against you."[9] The Word of God is a light in a dark world. It is bread, it is living water. The Word is the sword of truth. Paul calls it milk for infants and meat for men. The Word is a book of love, a book of mystery, of revelation, of hope, of prophecy. Do you want to know the future? Read the Word of God. The Bible is the greatest sex manual in existance. Sex is wonderful! Most of you are here because of it. The Word of God is a book of family planning. Most important of all, this book introduces your children to the living God.

Understand this, God is not a cosmic bellhop standing in the heavens waiting for your religious tip on Sunday morning. He is not a doting grandfather sitting benignly in the heavens approving of your godless life. God is a sovereign monarch of might and majesty. He rules from a throne. He has billions of agents coming and going, carrying out His orders. He is a monarch of judgment and wrath, as well as compassion and love. He is a God who expects you to do what He tells you to do in His Word. Jesus said, "And why call ye me Lord, Lord, and do not the things which I say?"[10]

Your children are not going to meet God in a Nintendo game. They are not going to meet him on ESPN. You, Father, are responsible for introducing your children to God. He gave you the assignment. It's called leadership. It's called being the head of the house. It's called being the prophet in your family. And someday He will demand a report on how things went.

As Prophet the Father Blesses His Family

In the Bible the blessing of the father determined the success or the failure of the family. The father is the spiritual authority. Father, what you say to your wife or children literally predestines their intellectual, emotional, and perhaps even their physical development.

- Proverbs 15:4 says, "A wholesome tongue is the tree of life."
- Proverbs 18:21 says, "Death and life are in the power of the tongue."
- James 3:6 says, "The tongue is set on fire by hell" and "it defiles the whole body."

That's the kind of power the Bible says you have through your words.

When Isaac was old, his eyes were so weak he could not detect his sons without feeling their skin (Jacob's skin was smooth and Esau was a hairy man). Jacob and his mother, Rebekah, conspired to steal the birthright, the father's blessing, from Esau. You know the story of Genesis 27, and how absolutely successful was Jacob's plot. Isaac, the aging father, blessed Jacob in Genesis 27:27, and every word of that blessing came to pass. Jacob was no sooner out of Isaac's tent than Esau entered with a mess of pottage, seeking his father's blessing.

Isaac trembled with rage at Jacob's deception. But note this: The blessing he spoke upon Jacob *could not* be rescinded. Isaac said, "I have blessed him [Jacob]—and indeed he shall be blessed."[11]

Esau begged his father for a blessing, and Isaac spoke a blessing that was more of a curse: Esau would live in the desert. He would live by the sword and would serve his younger brother, Jacob. Those three things came to pass exactly as Isaac said.

Years later Jacob, the spiritual authority of his house, blessed his twelve sons when he was dying and everything he spoke into their lives also came to pass. He was not just close; his patriarchial blessing was fulfilled in *every* detail. Father, your words have power—power to shape the lives and destiny of your children.

Every Friday night Jewish mothers and fathers bless their children. At the bar mitzvah they put their hands on them in front of the congregation and bless them. What do they say? They often use the blessings of Numbers 16, and they may add other blessings they want to come to pass in the life of that child. And with the power of the blessing of their parents, these children go right out into life and do these great things. They were given spiritual authority to accomplish it, through the power of the blessing.

How many fathers look at their children and shout obscenities? How many actually use God's name to damn them? How many call them stupid, cursing their intellectual potential? How many shout, "You'll never amount to anything," which is a curse upon their economic potential.

You are the prophet in your home. You are the spiritual authority over your wife and over your children. When you speak to your wife, bless her in the name of the Lord. When you speak to your children, bless them in the name of the Lord. What you speak will come into existence. Your blessing or your curse will follow your children and your grandchildren to their graves.

Dad as King

And finally, according to Scripture, the man is the governor of his home. He is king. Some men imagine that it is God's scriptural plan for them to sit in an easy chair and watch ESPN while their wives serve them lemonade, but that is not what a king is all about. A king is a ruler. Not a couch potato.

Why did God select Abraham to be the father of all who believe? Genesis 18:19 says "For I have chosen him so that he will direct his children and his household after him to keep the way of the LORD" (NIV).

That means you tell your children how much they're going to watch TV and how much they're not going to watch TV. You decide. You tell them who they're going to date, when they're going to date, and when they're going to be home. You do that. You don't hand them the keys and say, "When are you coming home?" You hand them the keys and say, "Be home at eleven, or you're not going out."

You determine what they do, when they do it, how long they do it, and if they do it. Quit acting like the wagon is dragging you. You're the leader.

Before you pick up the Bible as your textbook let me warn you, Dr. Spock didn't get to edit this one. The Bible calls sin by its name. The Bible tells it like it is!

American young people say, "I have a problem." If you have "a problem" in this country, you can get infinite sympathy. You can get counseling, and you can get endless attention. They will find you a support group. But when you say, "I have sinned," all you can do is confess and repent. This is the Spock generation and our jailhouses prove it. They are packed to overflowing with people who want their sins explained—not forgiven.

One of America's biggest problems right now is gangs. Some areas of metropolitan Los Angeles and New York are controlled by gangs. Police cruisers patrol like an invading military occupation force in a hostile enemy city. Who are the members of these gangs? Rebellious little boys who never learned to mind. Sons who were abandoned by their fathers. Daughters who were sexually abused and joined a gang where they have sexual intercourse with every male gang member to join. Their slogan, "Blood in and blood out!" The only way out of the gang is death.

The astonishing thing is that many of them, like the Menendez brothers, have fathers from well-to-do homes. I assure you that the only thing my father had to do to get my attention was to point at me. Just point. I tried to read his mind while his hand was coming down. I learned very early that there is a definite physiological connection between your cerebral cortex and your gluteus maximus. When you stimulate the gluteus maximus, your children will get a new revelation about who you are.

Father, you need to go home, turn off the television, and introduce yourself to your children. "Hello children, I'm Dad. This is Mom, and we're taking over this house. I haven't been very fair to you, children, but that is going to change. There are going to be some rules. At first, it may seem kind of awkward, even hard. But eventually, when your are thirty-five, you are going to love me for it."

Proverbs 13:24 says, "He that spares his rod," [and that is not referring to the family car] "hates his son, but he who loves him disciplines him promptly."

Proverbs 23:13 agrees: "Do not withhold correction from a child, for if you beat him with a rod he will not die. You shall beat him with a rod, and deliver his soul from hell."

A milquetoast father once said to me, "I can't spank my boy; I cry when I discipline him."

Then go home, spank him, and cry. Cry now or cry when he goes to jail.

I'm tired of people telling me, "I have a strong-willed child, and I just can't teach him anything." Wrong! I have been to Sea World where they can teach a porpoise how to play basketball. Surely you can teach your child to clean up his/her room, carry out the trash, and wash the supper dishes.

When your child comes up to you and says, "Will you buy me a little red truck if I'm good in church?" Tell him, "I'll give you a little red rear if you're not."

American fathers are saying, "My son's on drugs." That's a serious problem, but it's not an excuse for shirking your responsibility as a father.

I had a drug problem when I was a teenager. I was "drug" to church on Sunday morning, "drug" to church on Sunday night, and "drug" to church for the midweek service. I was "drug" to Vacation Bible School when I was old enough to teach it. I was "drug" to four revivals every year that lasted three weeks, sometimes four, and we went every night. I was "drug" to the family altar every night where my father read the Word. I was "drug" to the woodshed when I disobeyed. Those "drugs" are still in my veins. They affect my behavior. They're stronger than cocaine, crack, or heroin. Fathers, I say go home and give that "drug" problem to your sons and to your daughters, and America will be a better place to live.

Remember Dad, discipline without love is abuse. Never fail to put your arms around your children and let them know you love them more than life itself. As a father I make it a point to hug and kiss my children every day.

One day my son Chris got out the door for school before I could kiss him. I walked to where the children of our neighborhood were gathering to catch the bus. Chris saw me coming and started screaming as he ran from me, "No, no, no!" He knew I was going to kiss him and it was unthinkable in the presence of other teenagers. But I had to catch him once he screamed since several mothers were now on their front porches, hands on hips, ready to call the cops. Fortunately I was able to catch Chris quickly, kiss him, and get back into my car for a quick getaway!

In the sixteenth chapter of Acts, Paul and Silas are in jail. God sends an earthquake and they walk out with the jailhouse, keys in one hand and a convert in the other. The guard, who by Roman law had to serve the sentence of anyone that escaped, shouted in terror, "What must I do to be saved?"

Paul said, "Believe on the Lord Jesus Christ, and you shall be saved, and your household." And your household? Why? Because that answer was given to a father, and it's the father's responsibility to lead his household to God.

Don't send your children to Sunday School. Take them to Sunday School. They ought to hear more about God out of your mouth Monday through Saturday than they ever hear in the Sunday school or from the pulpit. If they don't, you're failing as a father.

Ephesians 6:4 says, "Fathers, . . . bring [your children] up in the training and admonition of the Lord." The word train is the Greek word *gymnot* from which we get gymnasium. God expects the father to show his sons and daughters how to live righteous lives. Just like a baseball coach would instruct someone on how to hit a baseball or a football coach would instruct someone on how to kick a football, God expects the father to teach and show his children over and over and over again how to serve God through their lives.

In the Old Testament Lot led his family into Sodom and lost them. He did not command them. And because of his godless leadership, they perished. Compare that to Joshua's statement in 24:15, "As for me and my house, we will serve the Lord." That was a command. Joshua didn't look over to his wife and say "Is that all right with you?" It was not a request. It was a command performance. Every father and every husband should look in the mirror every morning and repeat those words. "As for me and my house, we will serve the Lord."

Which brings up a very unpopular scriptural principle. The Bible teaches that the man is not only the leader of his children, he is the leader of his wife. 1 Corinthians 11:3 says, "But I want you to know that the head of every man is Christ, the head of woman is man . . ."

We talked about women submitting to their husbands in Chapter 6, now let's turn the nickel over.

A Man And His Remote Control

Some wives have a real problem. They married a Caspar Milquetoast who won't lead. Your wife can't follow a parked car. Some men haven't had a new idea in twenty years. They need to give the family some leadership.

The number one addiction in this country is not marijuana, it is not crack cocaine; it is television, and it is systematically brainwashing each subsequent generation. Television has become the nation's new guru. It is our religion. It is an idol before which every person bows. Today's new fathers were raised on a fictional television character named Archie Bunker. This supposed personification of fatherhood was a loud-mouthed, arrogant, ignorant, sloppy racist. He was held up as the stereotypical father figure. Funny, but at whose expense?

In the program *Soap,* the father was a weak-willed, vacillating stooge. The family received all of its direction from the homosexual son. That is the father image that is burned into the minds of America's young people. That is the look and feel of a "Dad."

Dinner used to be a great time for the family to be together. The problem is that in today's America, children gather around the television and watch murderers, rapists, drug addicts, and child abusers while the delinquent father reads the *Wall Street Journal* or the sports page. I want to give you a divine command from the throne of God: "Turn off your TV at supper and talk to every member of your family." You need to get involved in the lives of your children and the life of your wife. Your kids may be little people, but they are people with feelings and they are people with a future. If you don't get involved now, somebody will, and if that somebody is not a godly influence, you will lose your children and your home because of your own negligence.

David says in Psalm 101 that he watches carefully who comes into his house. They must not practice deceit. They must be in David's word "blameless." Yet, through the screen door of television you allow people to enter your home that you wouldn't let stand on your front porch without a shotgun in their face. These media invaders teach your children murder and rape and social violence. This intellectual cancer mocks your values and your faith. Take action. Turn off secular TV programs! Expel the evil invaders. Hear King David's admonition: "I will set nothing wicked before my eyes."[12]

If fathers are going to assume the role that God has ordained for them, they are going to have to have the discipline to turn off the television and get into His Word. If the fathers refuse to lead the family, the American dream will become a nightmare and the nation will collapse from within.

The Woman's Need

The Bible also clearly teaches the husband to submit to the need of his wife. He doesn't submit to her *lead*, rather, he submits to her *need*. The lead is his.

The Bible tells husbands to "love your wives, just as Christ loved the church."[13] And how did Christ love the church? Look at the record. Christ cooked breakfast for his disciples one morning because that was their need. Have you ever cooked breakfast for your wife? I mean, she doesn't have to have a 104-degree fever and be shaking with convulsions before the idea comes to mind. It doesn't have to be your silver or golden anniversary. Sometimes she just needs a break.

Jesus washed the feet of his disciples. Why? Because that was their need. It was a dirty job. What does your wife need? Does she need someone to help her with the dishes? "Boy, I'd never wash the dishes, I'm a man." Look, John Wayne, if soap and water will wash away your manliness, you need a hormone shot.

What does your wife need? Does she need you to go to the opera with her? "Opera! Maybe George Strait, but opera? Who wants to hear some fat Italian sing love songs in a language you can't understand?" But if that is her need, go. And I mean without dragging your heels in the carpet like a boat anchor. Does she need someone to talk to in the middle of the Dallas Cowboys–Washington Redskins football game? Then turn it off and talk to her.

I repeat: Don't follow her lead, but do everything in your power to meet her need.

Now I've talked to you about the role of the father and husband as priest, as provider, as prophet, as king of the house; but he is also something more. He is not only the leader, he is the lover. Don't laugh. They say that men who are bald in front are thinkers. Men who are bald in the back are lovers. Men who are bald from front to back, just think they're lovers.

The Husband as Lover

Now, here's what I mean by *lover*. Moses was the first king in Israel.[14] When Israel rebelled against God saying, "If only we had died in Egypt! Or in the desert! Why did God bring us into the wilderness to let us fall by the edge of the sword?" The whole assembly talked about stoning Moses. Then God spoke from heaven saying: "How long will these people treat me with contempt?. . . I will strike them down with a plague and destroy them, but I will make you [Moses] into a nation greater and stronger than they."[15]

Moses could have become the father of a nation greater than Israel. Instead he pled with God to forgive the people of Israel. That's leadership! That's being a lover.[16]

Jesus Christ was the King of Kings. He went to the cross and allowed himself to be crucified for you. When you love your wife and your children as Christ loved the church, when they know you are willing to lay down your life for them and submit to their needs without question, it will be a lot easier for them to submit to your leadership. It is not possible for an intelligent woman to submit to a macho Hitler in the house. You are equal partners, mutually submissive to each other for the glory of God so that your home can be "as the days of heaven on earth."[17] That is God's will.

Paul said in Ephesians 5:28, "So husbands ought to love their own wives as their own bodies." Go to the nearest health club and look at the men lifting weights. Watch them as they pass the wall of mirrors, looking at themselves with adoration in their eyes. When you look at your wife, she doesn't need to see acceptance, she needs to see adoration.

Whatever happened to romance in marriage? I read an article years ago that described attitude transitions in marriage over a seven-year period, using the common cold as the basis of satire.[18] It went something like this:

What happens when your married partner catches a cold?

The first year of marriage, the husband says to the wife, "Sugar Dumpling, I'm worried about my baby girl. I'm putting you in the hospital for a rest. I know the food is lousy, so every night I'll bring you food from our favorite restaurants."

The second year he says, "Listen, Darling, I don't like the sound of that cough. I've called the doctor and he's coming over. Go to bed."

The third year: "Maybe you'd better lie down a bit."

The fourth year: "Look, be sensible. After you've fixed supper and washed the dishes, go to bed."

The fifth year: "Why don't you take a few aspirin for heaven's sake?"

The sixth year: "Can't you gargle? Do something. Don't just sit around the house barking like a seal all night?"

The seventh year: "Stop sneezing for heaven's sake! You'll give us all pneumonia!"

Whatever happened to romance in marriage? I'll tell you. Paul gives the answer in 2 Timothy 3:1–2 when he says, "But know this, that in the last days perilous times will come: For men will be lovers of themselves . . ." Not lovers of their wives, not lovers of their children, but lovers of themselves.

I saw a cartoon the other day about a guy sitting in his easy chair in front of the TV. A football game was on the screen. Surrounding him were three cases of beer and 400 pounds of food. The calendar behind him read "September." Looking at his wife he said, "Is there anything you want to say to me between now and January?"

The most important thing a father can do for his children is to love their mother. Self-love destroys submitted love. Self-love is idolatry. It is spiritual adultery. Self-love says to the wife, "What can you do for me? You can cook, you can clean the house, you can bear the children, and you can satisfy my sex drive." That's not a marriage. That's not a relationship. That's not love. That's slavery, and it has no place in your family.

The Bible instructs the husband to love his wife as Christ loved the church. Love is not an emotion; it is an act of the will.

Husbands say, "I can't love my wife as Christ loved the church. I can't give up my self-centered life. I can't give up my pornography or my X-rated movies or my business career or . . ."

The truth is, you can, but you won't because you're self-centered. You won't give up what you want, not for your wife not for God not for anybody else, because you love *you* the most. That same cancerous idea is being planted in the mind of every child who watches television for more than thirty minutes.

A very meticulous man who demanded that his wife be an excellent, fastidious housekeeper, passed the piano one day and found it covered with dust. In the dust he printed, and underlined, "This needs to be cleaned." When he came home from work the next day, he found that his wife had placed a dust cloth on the piano. Good for her!

Effective leadership is not leading her your way. Effective leadership is leading her God's way. Submitted love means you meet the need of the other person whether they deserve it or not. Listen to that. Whether they deserve it or not. The Bible says: "But God demonstrated His own love toward us, in that while we were still sinners, Christ died for us."[19] Those who need love most, deserve it least!

A major problem is this. The husband sees the need of the wife, but his macho mentality says, "I'll hang on until she caves in." The problem with that modus operandi is that the little lady has a lot of spunk herself. She can get as mean as a junkyard dog. And then she eats his lunch. Soon, they are on the way to see the lawyer.

Rather than submitting to each other, they have demanded their rights. I have seen it flair up a hundred times in a marriage counseling session. I call it a "rights fight." No family can survive a "rights fight." If you start saying, "my rights" and "her rights," it's over. Call the attorney and get ready to divide everything you have. Let me ask you a question: Do you want to be right or be reconciled?

When you come to the Lord Jesus Christ, He says, "I see both of you, or I see neither of you. You are submitted to each other. Lady, you follow his lead; husband, you meet her need. Love each other as I loved the Church. Be willing to give yourself for her, unreservedly, with love that is extravagant."

Much has been written about wives who marry men with the intention of changing them, but it really works both ways. Many men think the same way. "I will marry her, then I'll change her." Read my lips, Leroy, it won't happen. There is not a verse in the Scriptures that says, "Husbands, change your wives;" nor is there a verse that says, "Treat your wife like your oldest child."

Now, let's review what we've said here. The God-ordained role of the father is that of provider, prophet, king, and priest. Wives, submit to the lead of your husbands. Husbands, submit to the need of your wives. That's God's divine order for our lives. And husbands, love your wives, just as Christ loved. There is only one way to handle a woman. Richard Burton sang about it in the Broadway version of *Camelot*. "How to handle a woman? Simply love her, love her, love her."

Make no mistake about it, if the traditional family falls in America, the nation will fall. If you cannot love and support your family, you cannot love and support the nation. If you cannot be loyal to your wife and children, you cannot be loyal to your government or to God. The fabric of the traditional family in America is being ripped to shreds by divorce, abortion, alcohol, drugs, child abuse, pornography, homosexuality, greed, and materialism. Men are more given to profits, power, and pleasure than they are the purposes of God and their family. The solution is God-inspired manhood. America needs men who will assume the role God has ordained for them. God is the creator. God understands us. And He can bring harmony to our lives if we have the courage and discipline to do what He says.

Chapter Eight

Deception
in Communication

Talking is not communication. You can talk all day without meaningful communication. Differences in marriages will never be solved until you have the courage to open up emotionally. Some couples reading this book have deep-seated problems in their relationships, problems that have never been addressed. Some are sexual, some are financial, some are emotional; but they cannot, or will not, open up about them. A crisis is in the making because there is no communication.

Other couples may communicate volumes without saying a word. They are sitting alone in front of a fireplace holding hands. The lights are out. No one is speaking a word but the electricity is flowing and the sparks are bouncing off the wall. Talking is not communication. The best communication possible sometimes occurs without words.

Have you noticed that young lovers rarely lack communication skills? That's something that develops after marriage. Usually, it is not the lack of communication but wrong communication that is at the root of the problem.

Communication problems in marriage date back to Adam and Eve, who had the only ideal marriage. He didn't have to hear about all the men she could have married. She didn't have to hear about what a great cook his mother was. When she asked Adam, "Do you really love me?" Adam could honestly say, "Who else, Eve? Who else?"

We have developed communication systems where men can talk to people walking on the moon, yet very often husbands and wives cannot talk to each other across the kitchen table. Problems and differences in marriage are not dangerous. But not being able to talk about those problems and differences is very dangerous.

In general, women have greater verbal skills than men. They express themselves by what they say while men express themselves by what they do. There is no doubt that when God passed out the gifts of communication, men got short-changed at least when it comes to communicating with their wives. Now, talking with another man is a different story. The only way some women can find out what's going on in their husband's life is to listen while he talks to another man on the phone.

The really verbal husband has developed a few words in his husband-to-wife vocabulary. The most popular one is, "Nothing," which he pronounces, "Nuthun."

"What happened at work today?"

"Nuthun."

"What are you watching on television?"

"Nuthun."

"What's bothering you? You look troubled."

"Nuthun."

Husbands who are riddled with doubts and fears are always dogmatic, and a dogmatic husband is usually an insecure husband. He can never afford to be wrong because he is emotionally weak. He has to dominate his wife.

If we husbands demand that our wives accept our viewpoint all the time, we are incapable of a vital marriage relationship. Understand, we don't have to be right all of the time. Someone else can be right part of the time. We are not omnipotent. We are not the general managers of the universe. We are not angels, even though we may be up in the air, harping about something all of the time.

When we demand that our wives (or husbands) agree with us absolutely, in every situation, we are denying them the emotional and intellectual life they must have to be a person. No one can survive psychologically and be so dominated. They will get a divorce to get away from you or find someone else to communicate with just to preserve their sanity. In the final analysis, they must have the opportunity to express their own opinions and deepest feelings.

Men say to their wives, "I don't want to talk about it. This conversation is over."

Read my lips, Bubba. It's not over. You'd better let her have her say right now, because if you keep it blocked it will someday all come out in a rush, and you're going to wish you had given her a chance to talk.

After years of counseling I have identified five levels of communication. All of us resort to these levels at different times in our lives. Sometimes the occasion or the person demands it. Understanding and identifying these levels may help us move onto a deeper and more intimate communication with the people we love.

Five Levels of Communication

Level One: Communication by Cliché

Here we speak in a very shallow dimension. Everyone remains in isolation. Everything is pretense. Everything is sham. We dare not reveal our emotional self.

Someone asks, "How are you?"

Of course, the answer is, "Fine."

They weren't really asking and you weren't really answering. The truth may be that you may have a 104-degree fever, and you are on the verge of convulsions. You are still going to say, "Fine." Why? Because you're not really communicating truth. You are only saying words.

Someone asks, "How is the family?"

You know the answer. You've given it ten thousand times. Now, the truth may be that your wife hasn't spoken to you in two weeks. She's pouting. You have three kids, two of them are in jail, the other's out on bail. But you say, "Fine."

Liar.

On the other hand, if someone asked how you were doing and you actually told them, they would pass out. They would be thinking, "Hey, I didn't ask for your medical history, I was just talking. I didn't really want to know. I have my own problems." That's not real communication. The first-level, communication by cliché, is simply pretense. It's deception.

Our society places a great deal of emphasis upon being authentic. But the truth is, most of us are liars. We place a mask over our real face, and we begin to play a role. Some of the greatest theatrical performances of all time were not played out on a Broadway stage in New York or on the West End of London. They were played out in the bedrooms of America. Many of us wear masks.

There's the John Wayne mask. I'm big. I'm strong, invincible, a man of iron. "I really don't need all this mushy stuff, Miss Ellie. I don't need all this huggin' and kissin.' I told you back in 1942 I loved you, and if something changes, I'll tell you." So she stops telling him. And six months later he is crying out. "She doesn't love me like she used to!" She didn't know he was lying. She thought he was telling the truth. I know a man who didn't kiss his wife for ten years, and then shot somebody else who did.

There's the messiah mask. Meet God's little helpers, the saviors of the universe, general managers of earth and all nearby planets. They are spread so thin doing so many good things, they have nothing left to give their marriage when they get home. They're so heavenly minded they're no earthly good. Be real! Be natural and let God be supernatural. Stay home and take care of your family and your children. Let me tell you something. Kissing wears out. Cooking never does.

There's the religious mask. You're so full of religious buzzwords, you're like a wind-up doll.

"I hear you're having family problems."

"Yes. The husband's left, but God's grace is sufficient."

"Your son is in jail?"

"Yes. But all things work together for good to them that love the Lord."

Hey, it's all right to say, "Things are not going right. We're in trouble." It's all right to say, "I'm hurting." It's all right to say, "I'm a Christian but I still need somebody to pray with me or I'm going to lose control." Quit running around, trying to act like the apostle Paul, when you can't find the book of Ephesians with a seeing-eye dog.

What game are you playing? What mask are you wearing? Take it off and introduce yourself to your wife, to your husband, to your children, and to the body of Christ. Role-playing is dangerous. It's emotional suicide. Why? When your marriage partner and friends change their minds about what role they want you to play, you won't know who you're supposed to be. In the process, you will lose contact with someone who's very important to you. Yourself! You will be lost! You will wake up someday saying, "Who am I?" And you won't know. You've worn so many different masks, pretending to be so many different people, you won't know who you are. The only guy who needs a mask is the Lone Ranger, and they've even given his mask to somebody else.

This special note to singles who are dating. People always wear a mask on a date. They have their best foot forward. Any nut, any moron, any orangutan can look good for three hours on Saturday night. Just remember, the real person is home in a cage waiting to get out. Date long enough to find out who this "perfect person" really is.

Level Two: "Just the Facts, Ma'am."

Most baby boomers will remember Sergeant Friday on the television series *Dragnet*. He was usually interviewing a witness when he would give his trademark line, "Just the facts, Ma'am." On the second level we start reporting facts about other people and what they are doing.

A wife said to her husband, "Did you see Mrs. Jones' new dress at church today?"

"No."

"Did you notice the Smith's didn't get the first row. Someone took their seats?"

"No."

"Did you see Mrs. Garcia's new car today at church?"

"No."

"Well," she said, "a lot of good it does for you to go to church."

There are four questions Christians should ask themselves before talking about someone else, especially if the information is negative. First, is it true? Second, is it information the other person needs to know? Third, what is your motive in telling your story? Remember, the Bible says that in all you do, glorify God. Fourth, when you're telling a story about a fellow believer ask yourself if it edifies the kingdom of God and blesses everyone involved? If the answer to any of these questions is no, then be quiet. It's deception.

"But I said it without thinking."

Let me tell you something about your anatomy. It is not possible for your tongue to begin to speak of its own volition. It does not operate by involuntary reflex. It has to have clearance from your cerebral. You say, "Sic' em" and the thing starts rattling. Don't tell me, "I just didn't think." You didn't think long, but you thought.

Level two is not self-revealing. We ask nothing of the other person. We give nothing of ourselves. It's empty, it's meaningless, and the sad thing is that the communication in many marriages stays right on level two, an empty reporting of the facts of other people. If it weren't for *As the World Turns, The National Inquirer*, and the sports page of the local newspaper, there wouldn't be anything to talk about.

Level Three: The Sharing of Ideas

On this level a couple begins to share some of the things they are thinking with each other. They talk about some of their decisions and how they were made. They may even touch on some of their material goals or dreams.

They are saying, "I will give you just a little peak at the real me, but as I communicate I will carefully watch your every move. If you raise your eyebrows or if you narrow your eyes, if you start yawning or looking at your watch or shaking the newspaper, I will retreat. I'll go back to levels one or two, reporting trivia. I will change the subject. I may continue talking, but I'm not going to step any further toward revealing who I am or what I honestly feel. Not now. Maybe never."

Those who communicate on this level need to be wary of two communication killers: tears and silence or pouting. Tears are used most effectively by women, but some men use them too. What are you saying? You're saying, "Don't tell me my shortcomings or I'll cry." In those first marriage spats, she will usually turn on the waterworks. She's communicating. She's saying, "This is the line in the sand, Sweetie. You cross over and I'll drown you!"

Many Christians have also mastered the technique of silence or pouting. They realize that it's not spiritual to explode all over the place, so they pout, which is only another type of anger. Pouting just may be the leading cause of high blood pressure, ulcers, and other diseases. And incidentally, it is a leading cause of divorce as well.

Level three isn't deception. It's just cowardice.

Level Four: The Revealing of Emotions

Jesus finally said to His disciples, "Who do you say that I am? I really don't care what they're saying on the street, but who do you say that I am?" This is gut-level conversation. At this level I am communicating the real me, what I feel way down deep in my spirit. I'm getting ready to open my emotional nakedness and show you who I really am. There's no mask here. There's no deception.

Communication in marriage begins on this level, without a fear of blowup, without a fear of pouting, without a fear of resentment, without a fear of being manipulated by the other person.

Level Five: "Symphono"

And finally, there is the absolute peak of communication, the symphony of the soul. This is when two human hearts begin to share their deepest and most sensitive feelings like two violins playing in an exact harmonic tone. Jesus spoke from this level at the Last Supper when He explained His death to His disciples.

The Bible often talks about the power that comes when any two persons can agree about something. In these Scriptures, the Greek word for agree is *symphono*, two human hearts beginning to share a pure and exact level of communication. There is no room for pretense in such communication.

The relationship with symphono has a beautiful sense of the presence of God. In that home, the angels leave the balconies of heaven and come to watch how a man and woman can be spiritually one. Here they can share the deepest feelings of their hearts without being crucified or belittled by their partner. Do you have that? Well let me tell you that ought to be your goal, because that's where real living begins.

The first step to *symphono* begins with a greater understanding of the feelings, hopes, and fears of your partner. I call it the "Ezekial Method."

The Ezekial Method

In the third chapter of Ezekial, the prophet describes his journey to an Israelite refugee camp near Tel Abib. Now, God has already given Ezekial a message to deliver to these people—a message that is burning inside him. But Ezekiel travels to the community where he "sat where they sat, and remained there astonished among them for seven days."

This is the key to effective communication, to communication without deception. Sit where they sit.

Ezekial was a prophet in a concentration camp for Jews exiled in Babylon. They were slaves and refugees who had lost their homes. There was no freedom, there was no hope. The Bible says they sat down and wept when they remembered Zion. Ezekial wanted to communicate to these refugees, so for seven days he ate their crusty, worm-filled bread and drank their dirty water. He slept with their lice and listened to their mournful songs. He sat where they sat.

Ezekial became a captive, he went to live with them, he let the blows of humiliation fall on his back, he looked at the world through their eyes. He saw a hopeless world where everything a man possessed was on his back. He sat where they sat. He felt what they felt. It changed his viewpoint. In his own words, he was astonished.

Husbands and wives can communicate in this powerful way. One of the most dramatic marriage encounters I ever conducted included the Ezekial Method. Some of the husbands were not very appreciative of the duties of their wives. One of these men was a macho orangutan who was totally unimpressed with his wife's role as homemaker.

"I'll tell you what you need to do," I said. "You pick a day, any day you want, and you stay home all day with your three small children. I want you to clean the house, while they mess it up right behind you. I want you to wash all the dishes, cook all the meals, and mop the floors. I want you to wash and iron the clothes. I want you to change the diapers. I want you to potty-train this little character right here. I want you to answer the phone pleasantly every time it rings. You get any groceries that are needed, and when your wife comes home at 5:30, I want you to be dressed fit to kill with a rose in your mouth and supper on the table."

He looked at me and said, "You're crazy!"

I said, "Hey, John Wayne, you got worn-out just listening to it all. But think about it."

Sit where they sit.

And husbands and wives are not the only individuals who need to adopt the Ezekial Method.

Doctors are wonderful people; a number of them are in my family. But I think every doctor needs to get sick once a year and be admitted to his own hospital, as a John Doe, in order to escape the messiah complex that most of them have when they walk into that hospital. They need to feel what its like to be kept in the dark while their colleagues confer. They need to be asked for their insurance card while holding their convulsing child in their arms as I once was.

They need to experience the joy of some female "Ironsides" invading their room at 5:30 in the morning cheerfully asking them if they are resting well while she sticks them in the rump with a needle about a foot long.

Every highway patrolman needs to receive a speeding ticket by some Kojak with a Kodak, who's been hiding behind a billboard all day with a radar gun while people are being raped and robbed all over town.

Every preacher should have to sit in a pew and listen to some of the dry, meaningless, long-winded sermons he cranks out when he doesn't study.

Every church member should have to sit in the pastor's office one week out of the year and prepare three original, life-changing, entertaining, yet theologically profound sermons—and do that while juggling life-and-death counseling sessions with at least twenty neurotics—run a day school, visit the sick, kiss the babies, marry the living, bury the dead, be out of the house twenty-eight nights out of thirty, throw banquets and a couple of formal dinners that week, write best-selling books, magazine articles, manage 480 employees, deal with the press, and juggle lawsuits—and still keep up with everything else. To this day some moron will periodically ask my wife, "What does your husband do between Sundays?" Such people need to try to study thirty hours for a sermon while the phone is ringing off the wall. I've often said, "If I wake up in eternity and hear the phone ring, I'll know I died and went to hell."

Sit where they sit.

Children have a marvelous capacity to enter into each other's world through imagination. I was a youngster at a time when every child didn't have two hundred different toys. There was no Toys R Us. We put a stick between our legs and a straw hat on our head and announced, "Hi ho, Silver, away!" Make no mistake about it, law and order had come to ride in the West. All crooks were in jeopardy. We had become justice. Children can imagine great things. This is also the key to understanding in marriage—to imagine the times and trials of your partner. Think it through and you will discover the words and the keys to healing and binding-up that relationship.

One of the most insensitive things you can say to a person in the hour of crisis is, "I know how you feel." You can't possibly know how a person feels unless you've experienced the same thing. You have to sit where they sit before you can begin to grasp the magnitude of what they feel.

Laura Hobson wrote a remarkable book titled *Gentlemen's Agreement*. This Gentile newspaperman was assigned to write an article on anti-Semitism, the hatred of Jews in our society. And so he took the name of a Jewish person and moved to another side of town where he could live as a Jewish man. Suddenly he found himself snubbed at all of the proper clubs because his name was not the right name. Once he was refused a hotel room. In one experience after another he was ostracized and shut out. He then wrote his book to express anti-Semitism in America.[1]

Right now in our nation we have what many people call a problem with undocumented labor. On a weekly basis I hear snide remarks about Mexican men who come across the Rio Grande to work in this country. Put yourself in their place. If I were a father in Mexico and my mother and wife and children were starving, you couldn't build a fence high enough or a ditch deep enough to keep me out of this country! I would be over here working any way I could. And if it's a problem, it's only because American men aren't willing to work as hard as many of those people.

On a recent trip to an Eastern city I drove through a ghetto where children were playing in the streets. In some cases, their parents didn't know where they were and probably didn't care. My heart was broken. Here were children growing up with a distorted view about what life can really be. It's deception.

If you want your marriage partner to have a change of mind, you must first understand what he or she wants and thinks, and why. You can't change an opinion if you don't even know what it is. Understanding is the first step. Then the tools will be available to make an adjustment. You may be surprised; you may be the one making the adjustment.

Adopt the Ezekial Method. You must communicate through compassion. To arrive at *symphono* you must not only understand what your partner has experienced in life, you must feel it.

Compassionate Communication

Ezekial already knew what was going on when he went to Tel Abib. He even had God's answer for them. But what he felt in those seven days astonished him nonetheless.

There are times when words are too feeble to express the pain of the heart. There are times when you go into a home and someone has suddenly and tragically died. The most genuinely communicative thing you can do is wrap your arms around your friends and hold them. Let them know by your presence that you love them.

There are times in every relationship when the only language that can carry the message is the language of tears.

When sorrow knows no limit, it can only be contained through compassion. Of all the music on the earth, none is nearly as beautiful as the music created by the symphony of two loving hearts in perfect communication.

Some who read this book will say to themselves, *I could have had a happy life and I could have had a meaningful life if I hadn't experienced such trauma as a child.* Others will say to themselves, *I could be happy if I weren't a member of a minority.* Such rationalization is self-deception. Jesus was a member of a minority and he lived a successful life, and you can as well, if you get the chip off your shoulder and start taking advantage of the opportunities that are available to you now.

Jesus, the crown prince of glory, came from heaven to sit where you sit. He was born into poverty. There wasn't even a bed or fresh sheets, just manure and flies in that manger. Jesus worked his early years as a carpenter's assistant for minimum wage.

Has someone accused you of being illegitimate? Every day Jesus lived, people said, "He's illegitimate."

Have you ever been rejected? Jesus Christ was rejected by His own people. The Bible says He came to His own, and His own did not receive Him.[2]

Have you ever been betrayed by a dear friend—not just betrayed, but delivered over to be killed? That happened to Jesus. Judas sold Him to be crucified like a common criminal.

Have you been falsely accused, set up by a rigged bureaucracy? Jesus Christ went through that charade. He was brought into a court and confronted with charges that were trumped up by the state.

Have you been falsely convicted in a fraudulent scheme? Jesus was falsely convicted. Pilot said, "I find no fault in this man,"[3] and according to Roman law the trial should have ended. But because he was such a cowardly, legal barrister and judge, Pilot allowed public opinion to rape justice. And Jesus was crucified.

Have you been tortured for your faith? Jesus was. They

spit on Him and they put a crown of thorns on His head. They nailed Him to a cross and suspended Him between heaven and earth. Finally, they buried Him in a borrowed grave.

How did it affect Him? Jesus forgave them everything. Even while He was still on the cross He forgave them. And He came out of the grave triumphant. Jesus did not say to His disciples, "Run for your lives. I never dreamed it was going to be this bad." Jesus said, "Be of good cheer, I have overcome the world."[4]

Whatever your plight, Jesus came from glory to sit where you sit, to know what you feel. That's why we pray to the Father, in Jesus name. Jesus knows the pain you're going through. He has sat where you sit. This is the key to pure, effective communication. There must be understanding. There must be compassion.

Finally I always recommend six steps to effective communication to those couples I counsel. This is the final way to beat deception in communication.

Six Steps to Effective Communication

1. Speak the truth in love. The Bible says, "Speak the truth in love."[5] Repeat that to yourself—aloud. "Speak the truth in love." Just keep this in mind: Truth is a two-edged sword. Be very careful when you approach your wife or your husband with it. The more truth you speak, the more love you should convey. Nothing improves your marriage partner's hearing like the sound of praise.

2. Plan a regular time for communication with your partner. I wake up in the morning bright-eyed and ready to go. I almost hurt myself rushing to the shower. My wife, Diana, doesn't warm up until 10 A.M. We do not talk in the morning.

Ladies, when your husband comes home from work looking like the matador who just got gored and run over by the thundering herd, don't tell him, "The washing machine broke today," or "The IRS called and wants to investigate you for the last seven years," or "I wrecked your new Mercedes this afternoon," or "I ran over your new golf clubs backing out of the garage." There is a right and a wrong time to break bad news.

3. Don't raise your voice. Prov. 15:1 says, "A soft answer turns away wrath." Here's the formula: Kindly, calmly state your objection in love, and state it only once. That's right, only once. Then trust the Holy Spirit to produce a positive result. You will never get anything changed by nagging. Be calm and gracious, and then be quiet!

4. Allow time for reaction. Remember, you've had the advantage of thinking about what you're going to say. You've prepared your speech. You've pondered his reaction. You have mentally rehearsed your encounter. You have said, "If he says this, I'm going to say that. And if he says this, I'm going to come back with something else."

He is coming to this moment unprepared. He doesn't know that it is all predestined, that you've written the script, he is already in the corral, and the gate is locked. It doesn't dawn on him. But the next day he can see it clearly. "I have been had." When he comes home from work, he comes through the door saying, "Let's talk!" What happened? You're hurt. He has changed his mind. He promised. No, he just caught on. It finally hit him. He's had time to think about it.

5. Pray together. When you start praying with each other and for each other wonderful things happen. You start seeing them through the eyes of God. You begin to understand them. And it is hard to pray with each other while holding a grudge.

6. Share the details. Men hate details. Women love details. It's been estimated that in a twenty-four-hour day, the average woman speaks twenty-five thousand words, and the average man speaks about ten thousand words. It has been calculated that the average working man and woman use about nine thousand words. If that's true, when the man and the woman get home in the evening, he has one thousand words left and she is just warming up. A successful marriage will close that gap!

PART THREE

Deception in Spiritual Beliefs

Chapter Nine

America and the Occult

My knowledge of the occult and satanism wasn't forged in a library. It didn't come from newspapers or books. It came from first-hand experiences that occurred over a period of a few weeks in 1971. My knowledge of satanism came from a literal invasion of supernatural powers that hit my hometown of San Antonio, Texas. It was like a chapter out of a Frank Peretti book.

Twenty-five years ago the *San Antonio Light*, my hometown newspaper, published a remarkable story about the rise of the occult in our city. Robert Pugh, Bexar County Director of Mental Health, was quoted in the article as saying that more than 55,000 citizens of San Antonio openly practiced witchcraft. Readers were told that satanic cult members were systematically performing torture murders, supposedly on orders from the devil. Pugh, himself, referred to three recent, separate accounts of murders accompanied by bizarre rituals. In one case a man had been ordered to castrate himself. And he did! Another cult member had been ordered to put someone's eyes out. When he grew squeamish and failed the assignment, he was driven to despair. Finally, as proof of his commitment to Satan, he put his own eyes out.

Only days after the article in the newspaper a very attractive, well-dressed, well-educated woman came to my office for counseling. Her family had sent her. They wanted to find out why this woman seemed to have such uncanny ability to control other people. As she sat down, she looked me straight in the eye and started talking. "I worship Satan. Satan is god. His presence is more powerful than Jesus Christ. You Christians kneel and beg God for what you want. But I ask the devil and he delivers, whether it's power or money or sex or curses or spells on my enemies. I can control people at my will with just pins and dolls." As she looked deep into me, her eyes seemed to glow.

I grabbed my Bible and began to read, but before I could get started she slapped at the book like a cat that was cornered.

"That book is a lie!" she screamed. "Nothing more than a pack of lies. Put it down."

You didn't have to be a Phi Beta Kappa in theology to know that she was demon-possessed.

I looked her in the eyes and I said, "Jesus is Lord and Satan is defeated, and don't you ever forget it. You and all of your pins and voodoo dolls can't begin to touch one of God's anointed children covered by the blood of the cross.

"You hate this book because it is life and it is truth, and you represent a lie. The Bible says that Satan is a liar and the father of lies. He has been from the beginning of time. He has no power in an environment of truth."

She looked back at me and screamed, "Shut up!" She just kept repeating it: "Shut up! Shut up!" She stormed out of my office still repeating the words.

I set there for a long moment and finally said to myself, *They don't really get into this in much detail in Abnormal Psychology Class 101, but what you have just experienced, John Hagee, is certainly in the Bible. It's on every other page of the Gospels.* At the university I was taught to believe that such experiences were based entirely on ignorance and superstition, but that was not what I had just seen in the woman in my office. She was deceived but not ignorant— a child of the devil who was obviously anointed by demonic power.

I had often wondered why demonic spiritual activity was so prevalent in every other continent except North America—Asia, Africa, South America, and even parts of sophisticated Europe, such as France. Accounts of such activity were clearly in the Scriptures and yet so absent from modern, American public life. I often wondered why the devil and his demons couldn't seem to get across the Rio Grande River.

Spiritual Deception in America

One of the most succinct fulfillments of Bible prophecy in recent years has been the rise of the occult in America. What began in the 1960s, as an amused flirtation with the horoscope, has now grown into a full-fledged popular movement with its own books and rock music. At night, psychics rule the television airwaves. Anthropologist Margaret Mead has declared parapsychology as a legitimate arm of science even while most state laws prohibit the teaching of Creation, even in private, church-run universities. Major news stories reveal that Soviet and American defense industries have been spending millions of your tax dollars every year researching the occult. The CIA even hired psychics to tell them where Saddam Hussein was hiding and what the Russians were doing. Police detectives routinely seek the counsel of psychics to solve difficult murder cases. The number one, best-selling books in the country describe out-of-body experiences and visits from the grave. Former First Lady Nancy Reagan planned the White House calendar with the advice of her astrologer. During his term as governor of Massachusetts presidential candidate Michael Dukakis was featured in *National Geographic* as honoring the state's leading witch. As I mentioned in Chapter 1, Hillary Clinton talks to the dead with the assistance of New Age psychic Jean Houston.

How did it happen so quickly? Wasn't America founded

on the promise of religious liberty? Wasn't the Mayflower Compact a commitment to God? Don't we mint our coins with the slogan, "In God We Trust." How could a country as sophisticated as America reject the God who blessed her and prospered her, only to embrace a renewal of pagan worship and occult ritual long since discredited and abandoned by modern man?

The generation before ours couldn't count ten books on the occult in the public library. Occasional publications on the subject were privately printed, but no reputable book company would touch such a manuscript. Palm readers lived in house trailers or shacks in the slums.

Then came the government's war on the churches. Prayer in school was outlawed. The Ten Commandments were ripped off the walls of America's classrooms. School Bible clubs were shut down. America proclaimed itself a new, secular society. The ACLU has aggressively fought for freedom from religion, not freedom of religion, under the shroud of "separation of church and state."

Into the vacuum stepped Jeanne Dixon, Edgar Cacey, and a whole new generation of psychics. Americans were amused. "It's only a game," they said. Horoscopes were published in the newspapers. But amusement soon gave way to fascination. "It's all in the mind," they explained. "Auto suggestion. But, hey, it works." Bookstores across the country began devoting entire shelves to the occult. Today such publications take up prominent sections of major bookstore chains. Except for the Bible, they outsell Christian books two to one. Year after year the psychic hot line outperforms all other infomercials on television. Make no mistake about it. Those numbers are driven by public interest and demand. Neilson ratings of these satanic infomercials reveal television audiences many times larger than the leading religious programs in the country. The New Age is fascinated by "angels," which are nothing less than demonic spirit guides leading their captives deeper into deception.[1]

The Rise of Satanism

While most Americans involved in the occult naively play on its fringes, some have taken it to its ultimate conclusion and embraced its most extreme rituals and manifestations. In 1966, Anton LaVey founded the Church of Satan. Two years later he wrote *The Satanic Bible*, and thousands upon thousands of Americans, mostly young people, began to flood into the new "church." From this cauldron was born a new form of acid rock music with lyrics of adoration to the devil. The Rolling Stones recorded songs like "Sympathy for the Devil," "Their Satanic Majesties Request," and "Goats Head Soup." (A goat's head is used in satanic worship. This is validated in Scripture where followers of Christ are "sheep" and Satan's followers are "goats."²)

Satanic Acid Rock

Let me tell you something. Most acid rock concerts are nothing more than satanic worship services. I've gone. I've seen for myself. When the mayor of San Antonio asked a blue-ribbon committee of clergymen to stand with him against the demonic influence of rock music, I went to a rock concert to see for myself. If we as clergymen were going to have a press conference to condemn it, I wanted to know firsthand what we were fighting. I was shocked and sickened!

I watched the leaders stamp the floor with the satanic salute and scream their oaths and sing songs that glorify drug use, rape, and murder.

"Oh they are just performers," young people will naively say. "They don't really believe any of it."

Not so. Some famous members of rock groups are on record that they have sold their souls to the devil for public popularity. They wanted to be as gods, receiving the worship and adulation of the masses. They wanted it, and they have it.

Former Black Sabbath lead singer Ozzy Osbourne sang openly of demons in "The Devil's Daughter." Osbourne argues, "I'm not a maniac devil-worshiper. I'm just playing a role and having fun with it."

Richard Ramirez, the Night Stalker, was obsessed with the satanic themes in the album *Highway to Hell* by the heavy metal band AC/DC. His favorite song, "Night Prowler," was about slipping into the rooms of unsuspecting women. It is no coincidence that Ramirez slipped into the rooms of his female victims, killed them, and then painted satanic pentagrams on the walls.

Dea Lucas, a high priestess in the Church of Satan in Van Nuys, California, claims that heavy metal is a prime recruiting tool for their church. "Heavy metal groups are influencing the kids to come to Satan . . . The groups are into satanism even though they deny it. Just by listening to the lyrics, being a satanist myself, I can read between the lines."[3]

The lyrics of current heavy metal and black metal bands are even more perverse and satanic, dealing with such topics as the death of God, sitting at Satan's left hand, sex with corpses, calling Jesus Christ the deceiver, glorifying human sacrifice, and the names of Satan.

You say, "Well, our children are just listening to music." Wrong. They cannot live on a musical diet of drugs, murder, rape, suicide, satanism, and doctrines of devils without damaging their eternal souls; and if you are allowing it in your house, you are liable for what happens.

Satanic Role-Playing Games

In the late 1970s new "role-playing" games popularized by Dungeons and Dragons began to appear in toy stores across the country. By the 1990s even Christian parents naively allowed their children to play along. This new generation of "games for the mind" could be played with a crowd or alone. The more advanced the games, the more elaborate the satanic rituals.

"It is only play, it is only play," parents protested. "After all, there are wizards, witches, and devils in kids' literature and the Bible." But these games were a far cry from the children's fairy tales passed down from Charles Perrault and the brothers Grimm. These were full-blown, illustrated textbooks on sorcery and witchcraft, including human sacrifice, ritual suicides, and sadomasochism.

Some young people couldn't get the scenes out of their minds. Several years ago, while conducting my own research on the occult, three separate deaths occurred, most of them within a few days of each other. In September of that year the body of a bright seventeen-year-old California boy washed up on a San Francisco beach. He was a suicide victim. Days later, a twelve-year-old Colorado boy fatally shot his sixteen-year-old brother and then killed himself. Two days later in a suburb of Chicago a boy and a girl, both seventeen, committed suicide by running the family car in a closed garage. In Arlington, Texas, a teenager walked into a classroom with a sawed-off shot gun, put the gun to his head, and fired. Finally, in Goddard, Kansas, James Kirby, a fourteen-year-old Eagle Scout, opened fire with a hunting rifle at his local junior high school. The principal was among the dead. Each incident had in common the complex, role-playing game called Dungeons and Dragons.

Satanic Ritual Murders

Only a few years ago, news reporters were debunking public fears of the rise of satanism. Reports of missing children were ridiculed as sensationalistic and hysterical. It was all reminiscent of the witch trials of Salem, Massachusetts, we were told. Today, one account after another appears in our daily newspapers. The satanic ritual murder of Mike Kilroy shook many Christians from their lethargy. Kilroy was a young medical student, kidnapped off the streets of Matamoros by members of what the press called the "Ranch of the Devil." In a ritual satanic ceremony his legs were chopped off, his spinal cord was cut out, and his brains were extracted with a machete.

On July 4, 1984, police found Gary Lauwers's body in a wooded area of Northport in New York's Long Island. According to a statement by police, Ricky Kasso, seventeen, admitted to killing Lauwers by stabbing him in the face and cutting out his eyes. Kasso said he screamed at Lauwers, "Say you love Satan," before the boy was killed in a satanic ritual that lasted for a period of four hours. Finally, mercifully, they burned him alive. As he was dying, Lauwers screamed, "I love you, Mother."

For several years Kasso and at least twenty others had belonged to a satanic cult called "Knights of the Black Circle." Kasso had an inverted cross tattooed on his arm and had been arrested the previous April for digging up bodies for use in rituals. He had stolen a left hand from a corpse. (The left hand is a choice portion of the anatomy of a corpse because satanists are children of the devil who will, on Judgment Day, be forced by God Almighty to stand at His left hand.[4]) My own research reveals story after story, too gruesome to print.

Some people say, "Oh that's a rare occasion. It only happens once in a while." Wrong. It's happening all over America, all of the time.

Today's crime wave of satanic murders or "sacrifices" is well-documented. Larry Kahaner, an award-winning investigative reporter who has written for *The Washington Post*, and a long list of the nation's most prestigious newspapers, has authored the shocking book, *Cults That Kill*. (As you probably know *The Washington Post* is not an evangelical Christian publication.) Kahaner traveled America from coast-to-coast, interviewing police detectives who specialize in occult crimes. The results were astounding. The problem is epidemic.

Kahaner learned that the moment of supreme power for a satanist is in the defilement of an innocent child, both through sexual abuse and, ultimately, sacrificial murder.

The sacrificial offering is considered the ultimate expression of loyalty to the Devil. And where do they get these children for ritual slaughter? They kidnap them off the streets. (Their pictures adorn the milk cartons on your breakfast table.) They steal them from their hospital beds. They buy them from drug-addicted mothers. In some satanic cults, mothers are required to give up their own children. An Associated Press story told of an El Paso woman who handed over her five children for satanic slaughter. She said it was an honor. Many missing children are tragic victims of satanism and will never be found. (It is no coincidence that the numbers drastically increase the week of Halloween.)

According to retired police Captain Dale Griffis of Tiffin, Ohio, babies make the best sacrifices. "Satanists believe babies are best because babies are pure. They haven't sinned or been corrupted yet. They possess a higher power than adults. When you sacrifice a baby, you get greater power than if you sacrificed an adult. One of the most prized possessions of a satanist is a candle made from the fat of an unbaptized baby."

Female satanists breed themselves to give birth to children for the ritual offerings. Doctors in the satanic groups deliver the baby, filing no birth certificate. As far as the state is concerned, the person never existed. But then, the state is not big on protecting children anyway—in the womb or out of the womb. The baby is ritually slaughtered, cremated, and the fat is used to make candles for satanic worship at a later date.

Police report that most bodies used in such slayings are never found. Children of satanists convicted of murder told police that most bodies were simply buried in graveyards, right under the noses of authorities. According to the testimony, cult members find a new grave ready for burial the next day. They dig another few feet deeper, bury the body, pack the dirt, and the next day the planned burial takes place with a casket lowered down on top of the murdered victim. Once the official body is buried there is little chance of it being dug up again to search for a second body. Family members owning the official burial place will not want their loved one's remains disturbed. The murdered victim is never found.[5]

The second favorite method is cremation. Each cult member takes some of the ashes home where they are scattered in fifty directions.

And why don't we hear more about this in the press? Kahaner says that police departments themselves carefully squash the stories. Kahaner was told by policemen all across the country that if the word *Satan* or *satanist* appears in an official police report, the attorney representing the accused immediately pleads diminished capacity or insanity, and the criminal walks "scot-free." After all, we all know there is no devil! Police are careful to keep that word out of any official reports and any leaks to the press.

There is another cynical reason why police squash such stories. Sometimes city politicians and police chiefs clamp a lid on the information for fear of diminished real estate values. Remarkably enough, some of the gruesome crimes occur in affluent neighborhoods.

The most disturbing reason why you don't read more about the epidemic in your local newspaper is because some publishers, city fathers, and even police officers are occasionally involved in occult practices themselves. They usually fear such horror stories will give what they believe to be "responsible occult activities" a black eye. But other times they are involved in the crimes and don't want an investigation. Journalist Kahaner was tipped off by numerous policemen that their profession was the profession of choice for a small, but deadly, number of satanists.

Who Is He and How Did He Get Here?

Students of comparative religion can tell you that the concept of Satan, or a "great evil spirit," is as old as mankind. Even the most remote, isolated regions of the world have had their encounters with the personality the Bible calls the Devil. They may have had different names for him, but he was always there. Pagan worship included self-mutilation, and there was always that horrible concept of human sacrifice. The Aztecs murdered tens-of-thousands to avenge their god. Revelation 12:9 refers to "that serpent of old, called the devil . . ." Old, because he's been around since before the Garden of Eden.

From the teachings of Jesus and the prophets we have seven descriptions of Satan. First he is a rebel. By definition, a *rebel* is one who always finds fault with delegated authority.

Satan, the Rebel

The Old Testament describes Satan as an archangel created by God. He was one of the three highest supernatural beings in the genesis of time. He was beautiful. He had great knowledge and great power. And because of it, he became proud and led a great rebellion against God, taking a third of the heavenly angels with him.

The history of this rebellion was recorded by the prophet Isaiah. "I will ascend into heaven," Lucifer proclaimed. "I will exalt my throne above the stars of God. I will also sit on the mount of the congregation on the farthest sides of the north; I will ascend above the heights of the clouds, I will be like the Most High God."[6]

Satan wanted God's authority, and he still wants it. He hates all authority. Even now, he is inspiring people to undermine God's delegated authority on earth, to undermine that authority in the home, as well as the church. Satan found fault with God's leadership in the Garden of Eden, and suggested to Eve that God was only being selfish by warning her against eating from the tree of the knowledge of good and evil. He was the inspiration behind Miriam's criticism and rebellion against Moses in the wilderness, until God gave her leprosy. Then she finally stopped talking. And he was the inspiration behind Absalom's rebellion against King David saying, "If I were king in Israel, we wouldn't allow this injustice to continue."

The teenager finding fault with his or her parents is in rebellion, and that rebellious spirit does not come from God. The wife who berates her husband is in rebellion to God's delegated authority. The church member who constantly finds fault with church leadership is often influenced by demonic spirits for the purpose of bringing discord to the body of Christ.

You are either under God's delegated authority or you are acting under the authority of the Prince of Darkness, Satan himself. You're either a slave to Satan or a servant of Christ.

Satan is not only a rebel, he is a master of deception.

Satan, the Master of Deception

Satan is exposed in Scripture as a "wolf in sheep's clothing."[7] The Bible also warns us that Satan is "more cunning than any beast of the field . . ." He is often likened to a serpent.[8] He sneaks his way into your life. He is suddenly upon you and attacks furiously and relentlessly at your weakest point in your weakest moment. When he tempted Jesus, he tempted Him with bread when He was hungry from a forty-day fast. He then tempted Him to prove He was truly the Son of God. Each time Jesus answered Satan with, "It is written!"[9]

Listen to this! Satan did not deny that the Word of God was true. Secular universities may deny the Bible is true, but even the devil knows God's Word is true.

Secondly, Satan quoted Scripture to Jesus but twisted it in an attempt to get Jesus to jump from the highest point of the temple. If Satan twisted Scripture with the Son of God in an effort to destroy Him, he will twist it with you to destroy you. Distorted truth leads to deception, producing false doctrines, division in the church, and distrust in the absolute truth of the Word of God.

Over and over throughout the years I've had distraught mothers and teenagers sit in my office explaining how it all began so innocently by opening their minds to parapsychology and to the world of the occult. Millions of people were seduced by the teachings of Jeanne Dixon. "It's only mind over matter," they would say. But in her own autobiography she describes the day that she lay on a bed and watched the serpent crawl up on the bed with her, look her in the eyes, and give her the strange power.[10]

Satan is a spirit, and when you open the door, he will come in like a roaring lion and possess you. Satanism is not a fad you can forget. Once you open the door, it takes you over.

Jim Hardy of Carl Junction, Missouri, began experimenting with drugs as a sixth-grader and was hooked by the age of thirteen. He and two friends forged a blood-brother relationship around drugs, heavy metal music, gory movies, witchcraft, and satanism. At age seventeen they committed a human sacrifice. Jim later explained, "I would kind of just pray to God and Satan at the same time to see who was more powerful, and little by little I fell out of God and started falling into Satan . . . You can't just dabble. It sucks you in real quick."[11]

You can't get rid of Satan with a psychiatrist or meditation. You do it through the name and the power, the blood and the authority of Jesus Christ.

According to Larry Kahaner, people join satanist organizations primarily for one purpose: to obtain power—power over other people, power over circumstances, power to make more money, sexual power, some kind of power. The satanists in Matamoros who murdered the young Kilroy boy wanted power to sell drugs and power to escape detection by the police.

The Bible teaches that Satan does have power, and he will give you that power—for a short period of time. All it costs you is your eternal soul!

Those famous members of rock groups who sold their souls to the devil have paid the price of their eternal souls.

"He who believes in Him is not condemned; but he who does not believe is condemned already."[12] So when you are channel surfing through the stations featured by your cable television carrier and you see one of these famous acid rock, satanic high priests spouting his lyrics of praise to Lucifer, just remember you are looking at a poor, lost soul who is only a heartbeat from eternal hell—not as some god, strutting his stuff like a peacock, but as an absolute idiot who has sold his soul to the devil.

Satan is a rebel, Satan is a master of deception, and yet Satan masquerades as "an angel of light."

Satan, the Angel of Light

Even while the Bible speaks of Satan's subtlety as the "angel of light," it warns that he can change his guise, in a moment, into a terrible creature. Peter describes him as intimidating and fearful, "a roaring lion seeking whom he may devour."[13] Satan will use fear to paralyze and control people's lives.

I saw how Satan changes his guise from an angel of light to a lion who seeks to devour that day in 1981 when the woman came into my office and announced, "I worship Satan." After she left, I sat there and quietly prayed. "Lord, you said that if any man lacked wisdom he should pray and ask for it and You would give it. And that you would give it freely. Well, I'm asking. Teach me the truth. Show me what you know that I don't know."

Then I opened the Bible and read the story in Luke 8 of the demoniac of Gedera who had been possessed by demonic spirits. He was in chains, the asylum of his day. He had supernatural strength. People were afraid of him. He had power. I read the story several times, not knowing that in less than twenty-four hours it was going to change my life forever.

The next morning I arrived at the office at eight. The telephone was ringing. A female voice on the other end asked, "Is this Pastor Hagee?"

"Yes."

"Pastor Hagee," she said. "I believe I have a demon spirit in me."

This was just too coincidental. I said, "Is that so?" Suspicion and doubt were apparent in the tone of my voice. Was my friend from the day before trying to set me up? I asked for her name but didn't recognize it. "You don't go to my church, do you?"

"No, I don't."

"Then why did you call me?"

"Because I pass your church every day going to work," she said. "I saw your name, I saw your phone number, and I just thought you might be able to help." She told me her story, gave me her address, and I reluctantly agreed to stop by and pray for her.

The woman lived in a very exclusive subdivision—not what I was expecting. I rang the doorbell, planning to leave if she didn't open the door immediately. She was breathless. "Thank you, thank you," she said. "I was afraid you weren't going to come." *She reads minds, too,* I thought.

We went into the den. She sat down; I remained standing. She said that her husband was a very powerful and important businessman who worked mostly in New York. She had dabbled very lightly in the occult, mostly tarot cards. It relieved the boredom and loneliness. It appeared harmless (Satan masquerades as an angel of light, remember). Nothing bad had ever happened until last Thursday.

"I was alone in the house, at about midnight, sitting on this very couch," she said. "I heard the front door of my home open. I could hear the footsteps of something walking down the hall, down the marble floor."

"Something? Or someone?" I asked, wanting to get that clear.

She said, "It was something. It didn't sound human, but it was certainly not a dog or four-legged animal either. I called out, 'Who's there?' It kept walking down the hall very slowly. I could hear every footstep. Then it entered this room. I could see nothing and yet at the same time I could feel its presence beside me. And then it entered me."

I said, "It what?"

She said, "It entered me."

"And what makes you think that it's still there?"

"I know it," she said. "My life has dramatically changed. My mind is filled with the most terrible and vulgar sex scenes. I have thoughts of violence. I find myself violently cursing people in public, people that I don't even know and have no reason to harm. Understand, I have never cursed in my life. This isn't me. I have thoughts of murder. Something is very wrong. Can you help me?"

Satan was showing his true colors to this women.

The Lord seemed to be whispering in my ear, "John, remember that story you read the other day, the one in Luke 8? Well, whip it out."

As I began reading the story of the demoniac of Gadera from the Bible, I instantly noticed a change in the woman. Her eyes glazed over. They had the vacant look of a cat; there was no humanity there. I knew I was facing something that the professor had failed to mention in abnormal psychology. I plowed right ahead, acting as if everything were normal.

"You'll notice that Jesus commanded the demons to identify themselves," I said, "and then He commanded them to leave. They had to obey. Are you ready for this to happen?" My voice was very calm, very clinical. But it was as if she were no longer there. "In the name of Jesus," I said very calmly, with no emotion, "by the power of His shed blood, through the authority of His word, I command this evil spirit to come out of this woman."

What happened next made the hair on my head stand straight up. The lady began to contort. She was a tall woman, probably six feet, and very slender. She was sitting on the couch but she reached down, grabbed her ankles by her hands, and pumped her knees up into the air above her head. Her head was now beneath her feet. She was literal-

ly bent double. Ten surgeons couldn't get me in that position. And as she went down, she was looking at me with
those glassy catlike eyes and exhaling a long, guttering,
chilling growl.

I thought to myself, *Lady, where would you like the new
door in your house, because I am getting ready to make you
one! It will be about 5'8" high and about 4 feet wide.* I had
never seen anything like that in my life. She slowly lifted
her head, hissing at me like a snake, pure hatred in her
eyes; then she spoke in a deep, baritone, masculine voice.
"I hate you, John Hagee."

I thought, *Hey, you know, we just met. It usually takes
people a day or two to hate me.* Of course, I knew that the
demon spirit was speaking through the woman. This was
spiritual warfare, and in any confrontation every fiber of
my being says, "Attack, attack, attack!" So I turned up the
volume and looked her straight in the eye and said, "Come
out of her in Jesus' mighty name!"

Throughout all of this I did not once touch the woman.
But if I had hit her in the face, she wouldn't have jumped
any quicker than she did at those words.

The demon's deep baritone voice answered back, "I
won't leave her alone."

I started quoting Scriptures. "Whosoever shall call upon
the name of the Lord shall be delivered."[14] "Therefore if
the Son sets you free, you are free indeed."[15]

After forty-five minutes of intense spiritual warfare, the
lady let out a bloodcurdling scream and fell to the floor like
she was dead. Moments later she sat up with a radiant smile
on her face. The catlike countenance was now the portrait
of peace. "I'm free," she said. "It's gone. It's gone. It's
gone. I'm changed. Thank God. Thank God."

There was no doubt in my mind that Satan had possessed this woman. He had entered her life through what
seemed a harmless pastime—reading tarot cards—and then
tried to destroy her mind, body, and finally, her soul.

Satan is a rebel, Satan is a master of deception, Satan

masquerades as an angel of light, and Satan is an accuser of the brethren.

Satan, the Accuser of the Brethren

The Bible teaches that Satan is the accuser of the brethren.[16] When you make accusations against a fellow believer, you are doing the work of the devil. Yes, stand up to evil. Expose the darkness. But God expects us to be forgiving and accommodating to the brothers and sisters of the faith. He expects us to get along.

James said that the tongue is set on fire from hell itself. You can murder another person with your toxic tongue. You can murder their reputation. You can murder their character and their influence. You can murder their marriage relationships by planting words of doubt and suspicion. You can murder their hopes and dreams. This is the work of Satan.

Satan is an accuser of the brethren and Satan is also a tempter.

Satan, the Tempter

Matthew's Gospel teaches that Satan entices men to sin. I remember talking with a young drug addict. "And what do you call the stuff you're using?" I asked.

"It's angel dust," he said.

That aroused my curiosity so I learned a little bit more. There is a drug called "ecstasy." There is even one called "heaven." But of course, when you get hooked, it's hell.

Satan is a tempter, and he is also a killer.

Satan, the Killer

John 8:44 says that "Satan was a murderer from the beginning." This is why he demands sacrifices. This is why he likes innocent blood, the young girls, the virgins sacrificed by the thousands by the Aztecs, and the babies sacrificed by the millions on the altars of Molech. His delight is the damage done to the soul of the murderer.

The respected historian Gitta Sereny, seeking to solve the puzzle of the monstrous crimes of the Hitler regime, writes about an interview with one of the secretaries close to Hitler, who saw it all unfolding. After many interviews, when Sereny had finally gained the woman's trust, she reluctantly explained that she had finally resolved in her own mind what had happened. It may not sound very intellectual, she admitted, but she firmly believed that Hitler had become demon-possessed.[17]

Detective Chip Wilson of the Denver police department told Larry Kahaner, "Where all these cults go bad is when people aren't satisfied to live within the environment they have created. It's not enough to have power over themselves. They want to control the heavens and each other. As the need for power grows, occult crime increases."[18]

Lieutenant Mike Davison, chief investigator for the Monroe County sheriff's special investigation unit in Michigan, reports other evidence of Satan as a killer—the cold-blooded murder of Lloyd Gamble, age seventeen, by his fifteen-year-old brother.

The fifteen year old called the police department and calmly reported that he had just shot his brother twice in the head at point-blank range.

He said his parents were due home at any minute, and if the police didn't stop him he would shoot them when they got home.

When the police arrived at his home, he calmly gave himself up. The police found his brother's body downstairs, shot twice in the head as reported.

Three days later, the parents called police and asked them to return to the house. When the police arrived the parents brought out a green vinyl bag that had been hidden in a closet. It contained a hood, a long black robe, a silver chalice, a dark blue candle, a glass bottle filled with red liquid, and eleven cassette tapes of Mötley Crüe, Black Sabbath, and other heavy metal groups. There was a book titled *The Power of Satan*, a paper pentagram, a sword, and an upside-down cross.

The book, *The Power of Satan,* came from a satanic group in Canada. The parents believed their son got the information about the group when he attended a Mötley Crüe concert. The book gave step-by-step instructions on how to perform a satanic ritual.[19]

Let me warn you. Satan is a killer. He doesn't like you.

"Well," you say, "what if I'm on his side?" There is no "Satan's side." If you let him, he will use you, possess you, and, if he can, he will then get you to commit suicide. There are not two sides. There is only one side, God's side; and you are either on God's side or you are lost, vulnerable, and in danger.

I am writing this book to serve notice that Satan is real. It was a very real Satan who appeared in the Garden of Eden. A very real Satan attacked Job. A very real Satan tempted Jesus, and a very real Satan has deceived the United States of America and most of its people. Some parents are fighting a very real Satan in their own homes because their children are involved with occult practices.

How to Fight Satanism in the Home

Most parents shudder at the thought that their children might be involved in satanism. And I don't blame them. Some parents even deny the possibility until its much too late. Instead I suggest that all parents be aware of the signs of occult involvement. Here are a few telltale signs from *Satanism: The Seduction of America's Youth* by Bob Larson, a man who has worked with young people for years:

- An unhealthy preoccupation with fantasy role-playing games like Dungeons and Dragons. You will remember that the twelve-year-old Colorado boy who fatally shot his sixteen-year-old brother and then killed himself, the Chicago boy and girl who committed suicide, the Arlington, Texas, teenager who shot himself in school, and the fourteen-year-old Eagle Scout who opened fire in a local junior high school were all heavily involved with Dungeons and Dragons.

- An interest in tarot cards, Ouija boards, and other occult games. The woman who called me so desperate that day had dabbled in tarot cards before she came under satanic oppression.

- An addiction to horror movies like *Friday the 13th* and *Nightmare on Elm Street*, whose main characters kill and maim.

- An obsession with heavy metal music, particularly black metal bands like Slayer, Venom, Ozzy Osbourne, Metallica, Megadeth, King Diamond, Iron Maiden, and other groups that evoke satanic symbolism.

- Withdrawal from church and a drop in grades. The child may begin to show a hostile attitude toward Christianity and previous Christian friends.

- An attraction to satanic literature and such books as *The Satanic Bible*, the *Necronomicon*, the writings of Aleister Crowley.

- An involvement with friends who dress in black, greet each other with the satanic salute (index and pinkie finger extended, with palm facing inward), speak and write backwards, or organize secret meetings.

- Drug and/or alcohol use.[20]

These are the initial signs of involvement with the occult. If you see such signs, you should be watchful, but as Larson says, "Beware of the temptation to search a child's room or screen his mail, which would breach his trust in you. Don't suddenly demand that every offensive poster come off his wall and every distasteful record album go to the garbage. Precipitous action will instill further anger and rebellion. Instead, be alert for additional clues of satanic involvement."[21]

Signs of deeper satanic involvement are:

- A preoccupation with psychic phenomena like telepathy, astral projection, I Ching, and parapsychology.
- An affinity for satanic paraphernalia, including skulls, knives, chalices, black candles, and robes.
- An inclinication to write poems or letters about satanism or to sketch designs of upside-down crosses, pentagrams, the number 666, names of the devil, or skulls and other symbols of death. (Examples of such symbols are on page 183.)
- Keeping a private journal such as a Book of Shadows (a self-designed secret chronicle of satanic activities and ideas).
- An obsession with death and suicide.

Larson warns parents, "If your child shows any interest in the occult, don't wait until there is a fire to set off an alarm. At the first sign of smoke, get help quickly. Contact a minister, counselor, or police expert familiar with satanism." Larson suggests that many public and private mental health treatment centers recognize the problems of youthful involvement in the occult and have excellent cult treatment programs. Their phone numbers are generally listed in the Yellow Pages.[22]

Every Christian needs to be alert to the possibilities of satanic involvement so that we will be prepared. Certainly I will never forget the last incidents in that couple of weeks in 1981.

Satanic Symbols[23]

HORNED HAND
The HORNED HAND is a sign of recognition between those in the occult. It is also used by those at heavy metal concerts to affirm their allegiance to the music's message of negativism.

ANARCHY
The symbol of ANARCHY represents abolition of all law. First used in "punk" music, it's now widely used by heavy metal music fans.

ANKH
The ANKH is an ancient Egyptian symbol for life and fertility. The top portion represents the female, the lower portion the male. This symbol supposedly has magical sexual significance.

CROSS OF CONFUSION
The CROSS OF CONFUSION is an old Roman symbol that questions the validity of Christianity. It is used on albums by the rock group Blue Oyster Cult.

CROSS OF NERO
This symbol represented peace in the early 60s. Among today's heavy metal and occult groups. it signifies the CROSS OF NERO. It shows an inverted cross with a cross anchor broken downward, signifying defeat of Christianity.

PENTAGRAM
The PENTAGRAM (without the circle, the PENTACLE) is used in both Black and White Magic. The top point represents the spirit. The other points represent wind, fire, earth, and water. It is believed to have power to conjure good spirits and ward off evil.

ANTI-JUSTICE
The Roman symbol of justice was an upright double-bladed ax. The representation of ANTIJUSTICE inverts the double-bladed ax.

BAPHOMET
The upside-down pentagram, often called the BAPHOMET is satanic and represents the goat's head.

SWASTIKA
The SWASTIKA or BROKEN CROSS originally represented the four winds, four seasons, and four compass points. Its arms were at 90 angles turned the opposite way, as depicted here, and turned clockwise, showing harmony with nature. The SWASTIKA shows the elements or forces turning against nature and out of harmony.

One Final Round with the Devil

By the time I got back to the office after my visit with the woman in that exclusive subdivision, I was exhausted. It wasn't yet ten o'clock in the morning and I already felt like I had run a five-mile race. In one hour my theology had been totally obliterated. I thought, *I'll never see anything like that again in all my life. I'd better learn what I can from it.*

But the day wasn't over. I was in God's classroom. I had asked for His wisdom on the subject, and He was giving me a heavy dose of spiritual reality.

That night a church member phoned with a bizarre story. "Pastor," he said, "I just hung up the phone after talking with a man who said he is going to murder me tomorrow."

I almost laughed aloud. Did you ever have one of those days? You had just a little bit more excitement than you knew what to do with? (And in the middle of the day, a couple, God's little helpers, called all offended because their name was misspelled in the church newspaper for bringing color toothpicks to the church barbecue? They didn't understand why I couldn't appreciate the pain of such a slight.)

I asked the man, "Well what did you do to him? What's the problem all about?"

He said, "Pastor, I haven't seen this man for twenty years. Look, I know this sounds crazy, but he's gotten involved in witchcraft. Every day he's in touch with some so-called 'witch' in California who passes on her instructions to him. She told him that I am the cause of a hex on his life. I don't even know what a hex is, but apparently he's convinced that I'm to blame for all of his problems." The voice on the other end of the line was sometimes panic-stricken, sometimes apologetic. "Can you believe me, Pastor?"

You caught me on a good day, I thought to myself. *Yesterday, I wouldn't have believed you. Today? I can believe anything.* "Get the man to meet me tomorrow in my office. You come too. Tell him that I can solve his problem with the hex."

The voice on the other end of the line was hesitant. "I don't know if I can pull that off, Pastor, but I'll try."

The next morning the two men walked into my office. The man who had called me on the phone looked terrified. I immediately opened Pandora's box. Why waste time? I looked his tormentor straight in the eye and said, "You think there's power in witchcraft? The blood of Jesus Christ gives every believer absolute authority over all the demons of hell."

He jumped like I had stuck him in the behind with a pitchfork. For a moment he was dumbfounded. When he recovered, he started in right where the lady had left off the previous morning.

"I know there is power in witchcraft," he said. "I can work a hex on any person I choose with voodoo dolls and powders. I can make bad things happen to people who make me mad." He was obviously threatening me.

I picked up the Bible, where the fight ended the last time, and said, "Satan is liar, and according to this book, he is a deceiver and a murderer. Anyone who follows him is going to spend eternity in hell, including you. Does that make you mad?"

It certainly did. He jumped to his feet, ran out, and slammed the door, saying very ugly things about my personhood.

The next Wednesday night I began teaching my congregation from Luke 8. I thought they needed to know what I was discovering. Of course, some didn't want to know. One lady told me, "Pastor, stop teaching us about the devil. I don't bother the devil, and the devil doesn't bother me."

Let me tell you something, that's a joke. The Bible teaches that Satan has come to kill and to destroy. You are in this fight, like it or not, and it's a fight to the finish. You will either defeat Satan and his demonic hordes through the power of the blood or you will be destroyed. Paul commanded the church to "fight the good fight."[24]

Fight to win! Fight with confidence! Fight with the spiritual weapons of Ephesians 6.

While I was teaching the congregation on this particular chapter of the Bible at a Wednesday evening service, the man who played with voodoo dolls walked into the church. He was carrying a gun, cocked and loaded, cursing God's holy name as he walked right up the aisle. He stopped at the pew where the man he had threatened to murder was sitting, put the gun behind this man's head, and roared like an animal. He took his hostage and walked him up the aisle at point-blank range and made him stand beside me at the pulpit.

"Now both of you," he shouted, "get down on your knees and beg for your lives. I am going to kill you right here."

I said, "This is the house of God. We are under the authority of Jesus Christ, and you have no power here. The Word of God says, 'No weapon formed against [us] will prosper.'[25] We're in charge here. You are not."

He started counting, "One, two . . .," and then he opened fire. It was surreal. He was pointing a loaded gun at us and firing away. We actually have a tape recording of that service. People in the congregation will sometimes play it. It will send chills down your spine. I promise you this, it was not a dull Wednesday night prayer service, and it was all on the front pages of the newspaper the next day. Not one bullet hit either of us.

That was twenty-five years ago. It was only the beginning of my new education about the spirit world. Forget all the ridiculous concepts of childhood, but believe this: there is a very real devil. He is a demonic spiritual being who can use people in an effort to control the physical world. His object is to destroy your heart, soul, mind, and body; to destroy everything that you love, everything you hope for, and everything you dream about. The Bible says that Satan comes "to steal, to kill, and to destroy."[26]

Every person who reads this book is either saved or lost. You are in one of those groups. There is no in-between. You are either sheep or goats, wheat or tares. You've either publicly confessed and received Christ, or you are the property of Satan. You say, "Preacher, I would never join the occult." Let me tell you something: without Jesus Christ you are as much in the occult as those people who murdered Mike Kilroy in Matamoros. You are his property right now. He owns you. The first step away from Jesus Christ is your first step toward the Prince of Darkness. When you reject the truth, all that's left is a lie and deception.

James 1:14–15 says, "But each one is tempted when he is drawn away by his own desires and enticed. Then, when desire has conceived, it gives birth to sin; and sin, when it is full-grown, brings forth death." Romans 6:23 says, "The wages of sin is death."

What is sin?

James 4:17, "To him who knows to do good and does not do it, to him it is sin." Romans 14:23 says, "Whatever is not from faith is sin."

Is there unconfessed sin in your life? If so, Satan has his fangs in your soul. No one ever recovers from sin without the blood of Jesus Christ. Hebrews 9:22 says, "Without shedding of blood there is no remission [of sin]."

Jesus said, "He who is not with me is against me and he who does not gather with me scatters abroad."[27] You can't be both things. You are either the property of Jesus Christ or a slave to sin and Satan. There are two lords: Lord Jesus and Lord Satan. There are two families: the family of God and the family of Satan. There are two destinations: heaven and hell.

The Good News

Now, for the good news. If you are a Christian, if you have committed your life to Him and been born again, Satan is a defeated foe. When Jesus Christ climbed

Calvary's hill He defeated the forces of hell. He became the sacrifice, the only sacrifice that is necessary to atone for your sins. Satan's power was broken forever. I thank the Lord for His shed blood. I thank the Lord for the blood of the cross, because through that blood we have victory and deliverance; we have freedom from sin and it's dominion. Every shackle has been broken. If you are addicted to drugs, you can be free today. If you are a servant to alcohol or pornography, you can be free today. If you are controlled by the wild emotions of anger, fear, resentment, or depression, you can be free. We have been made kings and priests, sons and daughters in the kingdom of God by the blood of Jesus Christ.

The name of Jesus Christ is *El Shaddhai,* the Almighty One. He, alone, has all power, and He has given it to us. Before He went to His father, He said, "All authority has been given to Me in heaven and on earth . . . and lo, I am with you always, even to the end of the age."[28] When Satan roars against you like a lion, fight back in the name of Jesus and the power of His precious blood. The Bible says that even the demons tremble in fear.[29] The victory is ours. The Bible says, "Resist the devil and he will flee from you."[30]

There is deliverance from Satan's deceptions.

Chapter Ten

Witchcraft in the Church House

Witchcraft in the church house!? Now you've gone too far, Hagee," you may be thinking. "Are you really sure the devil can operate within the walls of the church? Can he use churchmen, preachers, and laymen?"

Yes, the devil can. He does now—and he has for centuries.

Remember what Jesus said to some of the religious leaders of his day: "You are of your father the devil."[1]

Jesus made it very clear that at the end of the age the most subtle of Satan's deceptions would hit the church itself. He warned that his own believers were in danger.[2]

Let me give you some very concrete examples: the goddess movement within many denominations, clergy homosexual involvement, and errant philosophy and unusual manifestations of the spirit in the evangelical church.

The Goddess Movement

Perhaps the most stunning heresy ever to appear in the Christian church is the growing worship of the goddess Sophia. One United Methodist minister was surprised to encounter Sophia at his local church.

In 1993 Thomas Oden, a professor at an American theological school, attended a regular Thursday Holy

Communion service at this school.

The first hymn, "Sophia," sang the praise of the goddess Sophia, who "*ordains* what God will do." "She's the teacher we esteem, and the subject of life's theme."

Oden began to feel uneasy. *Am I in a place where some Lord other than Jesus Christ is being worshiped?* he wondered.

It didn't take long for him to realize this was true.

The sermon didn't focus on a Scripture text, but on an event in the woman's experience as a feminist preacher. She told a "victory" story, in which a "pious" Methodist lay leader and other members were forced to join another church after they challenged her authority to offer the Lord's Supper in the name of the goddess Sophia. She proudly described a sermon she preached to recount their disapproval, in which she invited all members who did not agree with her to look for another church.

The Scripture for this service was chiefly from the Apocrypha, Proverbs, and Psalms—mainly passages that deified wisdom. Then, incredibly, this minister likened the yoke of discipleship to sadistic and masochistic sex.

Thomas Oden wondered, *Can I in good conscience receive Holy Communion under these circumstances?*

The question was answered for him when the preacher offered the invitation to come to the Lord's Table, not in the Lord's name, but in the name of the goddess who was speaking through Christ. The congregation was invited to Christ's table, but in Sophia's name.[3]

Thomas Oden's experience is not unique. The goddess movement within the church finally catapulted into public debate after an international, ecumenical conference held November 4-7, 1993, in Minneapolis, Minnesota. Inspired by the decade long World Council of Churches celebration of "Solidarity With Women," the event drew thousands of participants from fifty states, twenty-eight countries, and dozens of Christian denominations. Twenty religious organizations funded the conference, including the Presbyterian

Church, the United Methodist Church, the Evangelical Lutherans, the American Baptist Convention, the United Church of Christ, and four religious communities of the Roman Catholic Church. The Presbyterians drew $66,000 from their "Missions Fund" to help sponsor the event.[4]

Not only was the goddess Sophia celebrated in open worship, but Jesus was roundly denigrated. Theologian Delores Williams, speaking about the doctrine of atonement, declared, "I don't think we need folks hanging on crosses and blood dripping and weird stuff."[5] A female professor from William Patterson College declared that the cross symbolized God as an abusive parent. The atonement was said to be a "wild doctrine that encourages the violence of our streets."[6] Two thousand delegates opened the evening chanting, "Bless Sophia. Dream the vision. Share the wisdom dwelling deep within."

Speakers encouraged participants to search their souls and identify their own "goddess" and not be inhibited by past restrictive traditions. Above all, delegates were told to "be inclusive." Participants named dozens of goddesses: "fire of love, she who is eternal, earth mother, spirit woman, yin and yang." A delegate from Union Theological Seminary introduced the conference to Kali, the Hindu goddess, Quani, the Buddhist goddess, and Enna, the Animist goddess of the Phillipines.

"Buddha died in his eighties," the speaker said, "Jesus died at thirty-three, maybe Jesus should be called too young to understand."[7]

Participants laughed and roared their approval.

A feminist from India anointed delegates' foreheads with red dots to celebrate "the divine in each other" and to protest the oppression brought to India by Christian missionaries. Chung Hyun Kyung, a Korean theologian, told the conference that "my bowel is Shamanist, my heart is Buddhist, my right brain is Confucianist, and my left brain is Christian. I call it a family of gods and they are all together."[8]

Sometimes the conference was not only anti-Christian, it

was anti-God. Chung Hyun Kyung took a bite from an apple, symbolizing Adam and Eve's sin and demonstrating defiance of God the Father, and asked the audience, "What taboo have you broken today?"[9]

Speakers also discussed the new sexuality. Roman Catholic leader Mary Hunt of Maryland reminded the audience of feminist theologian Virginia Mollenkott's popular quote, "Grace is a lesbian." In encouraging the delegates to become champions of the gay and lesbian agenda, she said, "Whether it is Christian or not is frankly, darling, something about which I no longer give a pope."[10]

In another session, Melanie Morrison conducted a "Lesbian altar call" while a choir sang in the background, "Keep on moving forward . . . Never turning back."[11] Hunt encouraged delegates to "imagine sex among friends as the norm. Imagine valuable genital sexual interaction in terms of whether or how it fosters friendship and pleasure."[12]

The most remarkable sacrilege of the conference was the concluding "communion service," listed in the program as a "Blessing Over Milk and Honey." The worship leader led the audience in a liturgical response, "With the hot blood of our wombs we give form to new life . . . With the milk of our breasts we suckle the children . . . With nectar between our thighs we invite a lover. . . we birth a child; with our warm body fluids we remind the world of its pleasure and sensations."[13]

How could it happen? How could leaders in major denominations be swept into such doctrines? How could some evangelical writers and ministers be seduced?

Sophis is a form of the Greek word *Chokmah,* used 141 times in the Old Testament. As in many languages, all Hebrew words are either masculine or feminine. *Chokmah* is of the feminine gender. In Proverbs, in a poetic sense, the writer personifies wisdom, saying she was present at the very creation.[14] Feminists declare that this wisdom—the Chokmah—present at creation, is the goddess Sophia.

None of this comes as a great surprise to students of the

Bible. Satan has always used God's own words to tempt and subvert His people. In the Garden of Eden he subtly misquoted God's warning to Eve, suggesting that God had put everything off limits. "Didn't God say, 'You shall not eat of *every* tree of the garden'?"[15] Of course, God had said no such thing. He had placed his prohibition on only *one* tree and Satan knew it; the thousands of others were available to Adam and Eve. Satan twisted God's words to discourage Job. He twisted God's words to tempt Jesus. And he is twisting God's words today to corrupt and deceive the church.

Of course defenders of the faith are in every denomination, people who have experienced God's power and who are committed to His Word, but more and more they are routinely ridiculed or dismissed. When a great host of Presbyterians objected to the Sophia Movement, Mary Ann Lundy, a feminist theologian, countered with the charge that there is a "battle for the soul of the Presbyterian church launched by political forces led by the far or radical right."[16] Many oppponents, not wanting to appear intolerant, backed down.

In the last three years the movement has only picked up more steam. In June of 1994 hundreds of women attended the Renaissance of the Sacred Feminine Conference at San Francisco's Grace Episcopal Cathedral. Again women chanted to Sophia: "We bow to your sacred power, the holy wisdom of Sophia, our beloved mother who is in heaven and earth."

A paragraph in the program said, "This participatory event celebrates and honors the presence of the Divine Mother at the heart of the emerging global civilization. The Sacred Feminine has a central role in the healing of our divided minds and endangered planet . . . Without spiritual transformation on a massive and unprecedented scale, human kind will not survive."

It doesn't take a rocket scientist to see where "Sophia" is taking her followers.

One of the many deceptions in the Goddess Movement—lesbianism and homosexuality—is also found in other areas of the church.

Homosexuality in the Church House

In many denominations, traditional Christian doctrine has collapsed in the face of the popular immorality of our day. The Bible refers to this kind of deception:

> "Professing to be wise, they became fools, and changed the glory of the incorruptible God . . . Therefore God also gave them up to uncleanness, in lusts of their hearts, to dishonor their bodies among themselves . . . For even their women exchanged the natural use for what is against nature. Likewise also the men, leaving the natural use of the woman, burned in their lust for one another."[17]

As recently as 1979 the Episcopal church went on record, condemning sex outside of marriage. At its annual convention it passed a resolution stating that "it is not appropriate" for the church to ordain practicing homosexuals or adulterers. But only a decade later, influenced by the cultural changes sweeping the nation, the church changed its mind. In 1990, Episcopalian Bishop Walter Righter ordained a non-celibate homosexual man for ministry in the church. When the action was challenged, Bishop John Spong of the Diocese of Newark announced, "This church of ours has done an audacious thing. We will not now tremble at our audacity. Rather we will step boldly into the future that we have helped to build."[18]

Then only four years later, in 1994, at the General Convention of the Episcopal Church, seventy-one bishops signed a "Statement of Koinonia," saying that "homosexuality and heterosexuality are morally neutral."[29] When conservative Episcopalians attempted to reaffirm biblical morality, they were answered by Bishop Orris Walker of the Long Island diocese who pointed out that many of his parishioners were single. "Is this church going to say to them that sexual intimacy for them is abnormal if it does not occur within marriage? If this church expects me to go back to the streets of Brooklyn and Queens with that one, it ain't going to fly."[20]

Conservatives were defeated.

In 1996, by a vote of seven to one, an Episcopal council of bishops in Wilmington, Delaware, dismissed the whole controversy with the remarkable statement that there was no "core doctrine prohibiting the ordination of a non-celibate, homosexual person living in a faithful and committed sexual relationship with a person of the same sex."[21] That same month, two gay men stood before the altar of St. Mark's Cathedral in Seattle to exchange vows and receive the blessing of the church on their homosexual union. The presiding minister announced, "Let their love be without shame, a sign of a new world of justice and peace."[22]

One of the great weapons of people in deception is the word *love*. The premise is "God is love," therefore anything under the banner of love must be accepted. That's wrong. Any kind of love that does not result in the absolute obedience to the Word of God is unscriptural and a deception.

In John 14, Jesus said to His disciples, "If you love Me, keep My Commandments." His words in verse 21, are very clear. "He who has My Commandments and keeps them, it is he who loves Me." Hebrews 12:5-7 is addressed to Christians:

"My son, despise not the chastening of the Lord,
Nor be discouraged when you are rebuked by Him;
For whom the Lord loves He chastens,
And scourges every son whom He receives."
    If you endure chastening, God deals with you as

with sons . . . But if you are without chastening . . then
you are illegitimate and not sons.

The apostle Paul tells Christians not to despise the chas
tening of the Lord. It is proof positive of His eternal love
in shaping our life and destiny. God never stops disciplin-
ing His children.

Look at Moses, at age eighty, chosen of God and com-
missioned to deliver the children of Israel from Egypt. God
sent him back to Egypt and on the way the Lord met him
and tried to kill him.[23] Why? He had not circumcised his
son, which means that he had disobeyed the sign of the
covenant God made with Abraham and his descendants.
God would rather have seen Moses die than go through his
ministry in disobedience.

Make no mistake, anyone who teaches "love" without
"discipline" is teaching a lie. Love demands discipline.
Anyone who tells you that you can have peace without God's
price of repentance is teaching you a lie. It is the doctrine of
demons pure and simple. Timothy warned that in the last
days men would be "lovers of pleasure rather than lovers of
God, having a form of godliness but denying its power."[24]

It finally took a pornographer to put the whole
Episcopalian controversy in perspective. In its December
issue, *Penthouse* magazine published an exposé of a "sex-
boy service," allegedly operated by priests of a Long Island,
New York, church. In an ironic bit of sermonizing the magazine warned readers that its story "may well shatter any
trust you have left in our religious institutions."[25]

According to participants, young men from Brazil were
brought into the United States by clerics to serve as their
personal "sex toys." The young men were invariably
shocked to learn the real purpose behind their exciting
opportunity to visit the States. According to one source,
sex acts took place before the altar, with priests wearing
their vestments and others dressed as women. The apostle

Paul warned the Ephesians that some "have lost all sensitivity and have abandoned themselves to licentiousness, greedy to practice every kind of impurity."[26] Paul wrote that their activities were too shameful to mention.[27] I know the feeling. But *Penthouse*, which has no shame, spelled it out in lurid detail, complete with pictures of naked priests and boys in bed together and stories of priests defecating on each other in orgies.[28]

If the Episcopalians seem to be leading the way down the slippery path to destruction, plenty of others are lined up to follow. In 1996, seventy-five Presbyterian congregations declared themselves "willing to ordain gay and lesbian persons."[29] Meanwhile, the legislative committee of the United Methodist Church has recommended that the church open the door to homosexual practice by stating it is "unable to arrive at a common mind" on the subject.[30]

The Word of God is not running for reelection. It needs no reconfirmation. It is a fact. No committee vote, no national convention, no trend, no compromise can negate it. Bishop Spong cannot save you on Judgment Day. Those seventy-five Presbyterian congregations will have no power on Judgment Day. The legislative committee of the United Methodist Church will not prevail on Judgment Day. Ten thousand bishops telling you that you are okay will not save your soul. Let no man deceive you. You and you alone will answer for your actions. And you will be judged according to God's Word, not man's word, not the trend of the time, but the eternal Word of God that never changes.

Finally, errant philosophies and unusual manifestations of the spirit are creeping into the church during these latter days.

Errant Philosophies and Unusual Manifestations of the Spirit

Satan's tactics are often a mirror of his own rebellion. He came to Eve in Genesis, saying, "You can be like God."

This temptation prompted his own downfall and he knows its allure. Such teaching is rampant in the traditional Christian church where writers and teachers are invoking New Age philosophies. "We are all gods," they suggest. Like the acceptance of homosexuality within the church, people promote this errant belief in the name of love and of helping discouraged people find self worth. And extremist teaching in the evangelical Christian church is a frightening parallel to this same dangerous philosophy.

Right now, in the evangelical Christian church, teachers and writers suggest: "You can be like God." After all, didn't Jesus say, "greater things than these shall you do?" Such teaching suggests that all elements of nature are subject to you. Even God, Himself, must respond if the formula is right. (He cannot resist your power because He has committed himself to those same laws of faith.) The result is that God is reduced to a genie in a bottle, obligated to our three wishes, no longer Father God with a sovereign will. If God is not sovereign, He is not God!

And that's not all. Other errant philosophies are also creeping into the evangelical church.

The Bible says very plainly. Do not consort with the dead.[31] But right now, in the evangelical Christian church teachers and writers are proclaiming, "I was inspired to write this book because I talked to my dead brother or my dead sister." It is often proclaimed from the pulpit. You can hear them on America's major religious networks preaching their gospel.

How did it happen? It is deception. It comes from an ignorance and a blindness to the word of God. It happens when we fall in love with the message of another man—not the Son of Man, Jesus. It comes from pride of authorship, when a teacher finds his unique niche and an audience approves. And it comes when experience is elevated above God's own Word. Some of Satan's most effective deceptions come from good experiences. When Satan can't stop you face to face, with his "roaring lion" act, he will come forth as "an animal of light" and inspire you to take a doctrine or experience to extreme. You destroy yourself with your own energy and enthusiasm.

Errant philosophies have crept into the evangelical church and so have unusual spiritual manifestations.

The Toronto Blessing and the Discerning of Spirits

Today the evangelical church is filled with questions about the "Toronto Blessing," a spiritual awakening that hit a small congregation of believers calling themselves the Toronto Airport Vineyard Christian Fellowship. It happened in January 1994, and soon spread across the world.[32]

Laurence J. Barber, senior pastor of Kingsway Baptist Church in Etobicoke, Ontario, went to see for himself.

> At one evening service, I began to feel a heaviness in my body, particularly in my hands and forearms, as though I'd just spent hours sculpting my father's garden hedge with old, manual trimmers . . . As I stood to receive prayer, I was determined not to fall down as some did, wanting to worship Jesus and invite his presence in my own way. But then my legs completely melted, and I fell backwards to the carpet for several minutes. My mind was still alert, wondering, until convulsions started in my stomach, and I began heaving sobs from the pit of my being.
>
> A sense of peace followed my crying in which I knew that I was deeply known, forgiven, and loved in the presence of God . . . Through my experiences at the Toronto Blessing, God has moved me beyond my normal comfort zones. Scripture speaks of many manifestations, like physical stirrings and shakings, that discomfit. Even though I was averse to them at the start, God has used them to humble me, reveal himself, and get my attention."[33]

Audiences were sometimes swept by waves of laughter. Participants defended the experiences, reporting that they were overwhelmed with God's joy, and laughter was only the result. There were thousands of conversions and claims of deliverance from former drug addicts. But soon, even more strange aberrations began to pop up.

Some participants began to bark like dogs, claiming they were under the influence of the Holy Spirit. Some crowed like a rooster, justifying their action by saying, "It's the dawning of a new day!" Toronto church leaders defended the activity, saying that the practice was rare and that it usually involved committed Christians who reported the incidents as very meaningful.

There is a cult of laughter in Japan where worshipers flagilate themselves with long-stemmed roses with thorns and roar with laughter. Take away the roses, and you can't tell the difference between this cult and some charismatic services I've attended.

Critics question the Toronto Blessing, saying it is unscriptural. Some even say it is demonic. Hank Hanegraaff, author of *Christianity in Crisis*, says that the Airport Vineyard represents something "extremely dangerous that could be a road to the occult" because of the focus on subjective and chaotic religious experience."[34] Ultimately, the church in Toronto was disfellowshiped by its own small denomination.[35]

George Byron Koch, pastor of the Church of the Resurrection in West Chicago, Illinois, also went to the Toronto Blessing to see what was occurring. His experience was different from Laurence Barber's.

After a time of praise and worship choruses, announcements, and preaching, an invitation to receive prayer and the Blessing was given, and authorized prayer ministers moved through the crowd, using trademark gestures:

One minister stood behind a couple who wanted prayer for their struggle with infertility. He held his hands above their heads, palms downward, and began pumping vigorously up and down, as if pushing something into them.

Another minister stood in front of a man desiring prayer, resting his left hand on the man while scooping the air in a sideways motion with his right hand, as if pulling something out of the air and into the man's body.

Eventually, this man and others fell to the floor to "rest in the Spirit." As the minister moved on, he occasionally looked back at those on the floor and scooped his hand through the air again, lightly throwing "something" toward them.

Other ministers blew on those being prayed for with a series of quick breaths."[36]

George Koch is an evangelical charismatic who accepts phenomenal gifts of the Holy Spirit yet he says, "What I found at the Airport Vineyard is an apparent theology of the Holy Spirit, on the part of some ministers and others involved in the worship, that is both unorthodox and potentially much more serious than the phenomena on the fringe of the worship."[37]

Koch says that the churches to which the Blessing has spread "should move quickly to give clear, regular, and thorough teaching on the person of the Holy Spirit to ministers and congregations. It may even be that some of the more bizarre phenomena will flee when those involved acknowledge the person and sovereignty of the Holy Spirit, invite him in, and rebuke and renounce any other 'power' that any individual might personally control."[38]

In these latter days, each Christian needs to ask himself: What is of God? What is a deception? How can I discern the difference? Hear this! If you laugh because you are happy, it can be a manifestation of the Holy Spirit because "the fruit of the Spirit is joy."[39] If you are laughing to become happy, this is a manipulation of emotion, which is witchcraft.

Testing Spiritual Experiences

The first question that must be asked when a supernatural manifestation happens in the church or in the life of a believer is this: "Is the manifestation of the Holy Spirit, is it sensual or ego driven, or is it demonic?" Every manifestation comes from one of these three sources.

Many readers may be shocked by the concept that a demon spirit could manifest itself in a church worship environment. Yet some of the most powerful demon manifestations I have ever seen happened while I was preaching the Word of God. In the last chapter I described a man, claiming to be under the influence of a witch, who strode into our church with a loaded pistol, intending to shoot me before the congregation.

I am alive today because of the supernatural power of God to protect and defend the righteous. Satan hates the Word of God! It has the ability to expose him and the power to cast him out of believers and out of the church. But make no mistake, Satan can operate in a church worship setting. The Bible says we must "test the spirits."[40]

Some Christians who are caught up in supernatural manifestations will teach that it is a sign of ungratefulness or a lack of faith to question or test what is happening. "Just open up to it," they will urge. "Just receive it."

Hold on. That is plainly contrary to the Word of God. Paul warns the early Christians: "Test all things; hold fast what is good."[41] Teaching that discourages testing of doctrines and experiences and is in violation of Scripture.

Unfortunately when some people don't receive these manifestations, those who do label them "hard to receive." The message? You're not as spiritual as we are, which is Pharisaism!

Our hearts and emotions are not a valid basis of truth. Proverbs 28:26 states, "He who trusts in his own heart is a fool." Do not rely on what your heart tells you because it is not reliable. Jeremiah writes in 17:19: "The heart is deceitful above all things, and desperately wicked, who can know it." I have heard many people justify manifestations based on their emotions, their feelings, or their experiences. This is quicksand. Only the Word of God is a valid foundation for what you believe.

The difficulty with supernatural manifestations in the church is the ability of believers to discern between manifestations. I have been in church services where a bona fide manifestation of the Holy Spirit was occurring in one person's life and on the same pew another person was manifesting a demon spirit.

King Saul is the perfect illustration of this mixture. Saul ruled Israel for forty years. He was a successful military commander. But his life was destroyed because he allowed a mixture of spirits to rule his life. The Bible records the same man prophesying under the influence of the Holy Spirit and later prophesying under the influence of a demon. On the last night of his life, he went to consult the witch in the cave of Endore. The next day he committed suicide on the battlefield.

A mixture of spirits will destroy a man and any church where it's permitted.

Such a mixture will produce two things: confusion and then division. A woman came into my church who had visited one of the highly publicized revivals where manifestations are apparently rampant. Her first Sunday back at Cornerstone Church, she sat in the pew during the song service and shook both hands in the air violently as though swatting at a horde of invisible bees. Although she was in the balcony, I had the ushers escort her out of the service. She was out of order.

Every pastor in every church in America should escort anyone out of the service whose bizarre behavior or manifestations attract attention so exclusively to them that the service and worship of other people is disrupted. For a pastor to allow anyone's personal manifestation to destroy a worship service is a dereliction of duty.

Because I had the woman ushered out, some who thought of the woman as deeply spiritual, were now confused. Others rejected her personally, which is division. I repeat, a mixture of spirits produces confusion and division.

The Bible gives us no liberty to tolerate the intrusion of evil into the church. We are not to be passive; we are not to be neutral. Proverbs 8:13 says, "The fear of the Lord is to hate evil." It is sinful to be neutral toward evil. Jesus said in Matthew 12:30, "He who is not with Me is against Me." There is no room for neutrality.

I have this word of warning for the church: Any "manifestation of the spirit" that prohibits the preaching of the Word of God on a regular basis is not from God. Satan hates the Word. If he can fill the House of God with confusion, created by an aberrant supernatural manifestation, and stop the preaching of the Word of God, he will do it!

George Koch was right when he said churches "should move to give clear, regular, and thorough teaching on the person of the Holy Spirit." A public manifestation is either from the Holy Spirit, which is acceptable, from the person themselves—a human, sensual act—or from a demon spirit. The latter two are unacceptable.

How then do we recognize the Holy Spirit? There are three clues.

Recognizing the Holy Spirit

1. If a spirit is used for control or manipulation, even of a congregation, it is not the Holy Spirit. The Holy Spirit is God, and no one uses God. One of the great dangers of those who minister in the supernatural realm is the temptation to use spiritual gifts to dominate people. This is the spirit of witchcraft, not the Holy Spirit.

2. The Holy Spirit is the servant of God, the Father, and God, the Son. This is an exciting revelation because it gives

such a high value to servanthood. Think of it, one form of God, Himself, is that of a servant. Unfortunately many people today despise the idea of servanthood.

In John 16:13-14 Jesus gives us a glimpse of the Holy Spirit's ministry and activity: "However, when He, the Spirit of Truth, has come, He will guide you into all truth; for He will not speak on His own authority, but whatever He hears He will speak; and He will tell you things to come. He will glorify Me, for He will take of what is Mine and declare it to you."

The Holy Spirit does not speak for Himself. He has no message of His own. He only reports to us what He is hearing from God, the Father, and God, the Son. His aim is not to glorify Himself but to bring glory to Jesus Christ. Anything that brings glory to a man will eventually lead to deception. When you hear a soloist sing a mighty song of the church do you say, "What a great singer" or "What a great Savior?" It is proper to "give honor to whom honor is due," but glory alone belongs to God.

3. By His very name, He is holy. In Hebrew, He is *the Spirit of Holiness.* Most "cafeteria Christians," those Christians who pick and chose the doctrines they want, consider holiness optional. It is not!

In Hebrews 12:14 the writer says, "Pursue peace with all people, and holiness, without which no man shall see the Lord."

Ministers who manipulate audiences with hype or psychic powers, pretending to do so under the auspices of the Holy Spirit, are in grave danger. Jesus warns in Matthew 12:31-32, "Therefore I say unto you, every sin and blasphemy will be forgiven men, but the blasphemy against the Spirit will not be forgiven men. Anyone who speaks a word against the Son of Man, it will be forgiven him; but whoever speaks against the Holy Spirit it will not be forgiven him, either in this age or in the age to come."

Jesus gives this frightening warning Himself. Beware how we speak about the Holy Spirit and how we represent the Holy Spirit. Jesus uses the word *blasphemy* whose primary meaning is "to speak lightly or amiss of sacred things." When you speak lightly or amiss of the Holy Spirit you are by definition practicing blasphemy.

Today, many Christians are far more interested in signs and wonders than they are the preaching of the Cross. Hear this! Signs and wonders do not determine truth! Truth is determined by the Word of God. In John 17:17, Jesus is praying to the Father, and He says, "Your Word is Truth." It's not trying to be truth, it is truth.

Signs and wonders will be the forte of the Antichrist. The apostle Paul warns the Thessalonians:

> The coming of the lawless one (the Antichrist) is according to the working of Satan, with all power, signs, and lying wonders, and with all unrighteous deception among those who perish, because they did not receive the love of the truth, that they might be saved. And for this reason God will send them a strong delusion, that they should believe a lie, that they all may be condemned who did not believe the truth but had pleasure in unrighteousness.[42]

What happens to the man, the church, or the denomination that will not receive "the love of the truth?" Paul states that God sends them a strong delusion. This severe judgment will happen to any person who allows his relationship with God to be controlled by his opinions (which is intellectual idolatry), by his emotions, or by experiences that are not in harmony with the Word of God.

Besides a true knowledge of the Holy Spirit, we have another scriptural antidote to deception in the church in these latter days.

The Antidote to Deception

Christians must maintain an eternal perspective, rather than an earthly one where our vision is completely limited to the here and now. If all we are expecting from God through salvation are things that belong to this life—prosperity, healing, success, and power—we will never reach our spiritual destiny.

Abraham is the prime example of a believer who maintained an eternal perspective and was not limited to an earthly perspective. In Hebrews 11:9-10, speaking about Abraham, the Bible says:

> By faith he dwelt in the land of promise as in a foreign country, dwelling in tents with Isaac and Jacob, the heirs with him of the same promise; for he waited for a city which has foundations, whose builder and maker is God.

Abraham was in the Promised Land, it was promised to him and given to him by God through a blood covenant, but he never lived there as if he owned it. He always lived in a tent. He never bought a house. Abraham had a vision that extended beyond time into eternity. I believe this is how God expects Christians to be. We are not at home in this world. Our citizenship is in heaven. When we become at home in this world, we become soulish. "Do not love the world or the things in the world. If any one loves the world, the love of the father is not in him."[43]

Compare Lot to Abraham. Lot looked towards Sodom, and the next thing we read is that he is not just looking towards Sodom, he is in Sodom; he is living in a house, no longer a tent. He is the type of earthly man of God who ceased to see the eternal and almost lost his soul.

Moses never lost sight of the eternal. Hebrews 11:27 states: "By faith he forsook Egypt, not fearing the wrath of the king; for he endured as seeing Him who is invisible."

The key for victorious Christian living is to never lose sight of the eternal. Look beyond time. Look beyond the burden you carry. Look beyond the present into God's tomorrow. Test the spirits to see if they are of God. Stay rooted in the Scriptures. Work out your own salvation as the Bible says "in fear and trembling."

PART FOUR

Truth Over Deception

Chapter Eleven

Deliverance from Deception

A ll right," you say. "I give up. Compared to the strict standard of God's Word, America is indeed living in deception." Our government pretends to be democratic, but has been co-opted by a clique of willfull, anti-Christian bigots, bent on discrediting God's Word and God's people, only to justify their own immorality. Some are bureaucrats. Most are judges, ruling America by fiat.

Think about this! When one branch of the federal government makes the laws, enforces the laws, and interprets the laws you have a dictatorship.

When Hitler did this in Germany, it was called Nazism. When the Bolsheviks in Russia did this, it was called communism. When America's activist judges do this, it's called "compassion" for a people too incompetent for self-rule.

- When the people of California voted against Proposition 209, stating there would be no more affirmative action, the federal judge overturned the will of the people calling it unconstitutional.

- As this book goes to print the Hawaiian Circuit Court has ignored a mountain of evidence that homosexuality is destrutive to individuals, families, and societies by striking down a Hawaii state law that preserves marriage as a union between one man and one woman. Once again, the liberal court has ignored the will of the people who voted overwhelmingly in recent elections to support marriage.

The vote of the people no longer matters. Politicians wonder why more American people don't vote. The simple answer is if the will of the people differs with a federal judge, the will of the people means nothing.

The Battle Against Deception

Three God-given weapons can bring deliverance from deception. Three weapons can cut through the fog. One is praise, one is faith, and the last is action.

It isn't good enough to believe in God's Word and agree that the philosophy of this age has been corrupted. The demons themselves tremble and believe.[1] The Bible says that "faith without works is dead."[2] In His challenging Sermon on the Mount, Jesus didn't call for believers. He didn't say that the wise man would believe Him. He said that the wise man, the man who built his house on a rock would *do* what Jesus had commanded. It is what we *do* that will break Satan's hold on our life and our nation. It is time to go to work.

"But what can I do?" people ask me. "I am one person. How can I stem the tide of corruption in Washington? What can I do to restore marriage values to American homes? I'm not even a preacher, so how am I supposed to influence the direction of my church?"

God does not demand results, He demands obedience and action. He expects us to be faithful. When the angel of the Lord appeared to Gideon he came with this solemn charge, "Go in this might of yours, and you shall save Israel."[3] Gideon was flabbergasted. This angel apparently didn't know who he was talking to.

Gideon was thinking, *If I could do something I would have done it a long time ago. I am too weak. I can't. Our enemies have oppressed us for years. Only God can change that . . .*

What is this? Why are you telling me to go save my country? Gideon told the angel that he was the least family member, in the least family, in the least tribe, in all of Israel.

But God said go. And he did not just say go. He said, "Go in your power."

All of us have power. It may not be much. But God wants it. He wants us to use it, to exercise it. He wants us to give it to Him so He can bless it and put it to work. The Bible says that God will judge the nations. We will be judged as Americans. We will have to give account for what happened to our country on our watch. On *our* watch. What will we say to Him?

"We couldn't do anything, so we did nothing"?

He will say, "You had the freedom to petition government. Did you write your senator, your congressman, your judges, your president? You had freedom of the press. What did you publish? You had freedom to speak. There were people dying all around you. What did you say?"

And we will say, "But I didn't think that my letter would make a difference."

God does not expect us to change the world. He does, however, expect us to be obedient.

"I agree," you say. "The American family has been hijacked by a selfish, do-what-makes-you-feel-good, hedonistic philosophy that has already proven its destructiveness by unleashing a wave of venereal disease, unwanted pregnancies, and tragic divorces, poisoning a second and third generation to come. No one even questions that philosophy. As bankrupt as it may be, it is considered the gospel to this end-times generation. To challenge it is to be considered ignorant or reactionary.

"And yes," you say, "even the Christian church has fallen prey to Satan's deceptions. As preposterous as it sounds to people about to enter the twenty-first century, church leaders are reviving ancient forms of idol worship and worship of nature and bringing into the sanctuary rituals and sorcery that God punished Israel for thousands of years ago.

"Yes, America is deceived. But so what? What can I do about it? What can anyone do about it? Anyway, didn't Jesus say something exactly like this would happen?"

There are biblical answers to all of those questions but first listen closely to the warning Jesus gave that peaceful afternoon on the Mount of Olives two thousand years ago. "Let no man deceive you. Let no man deceive you." Don't let it happen. Stop it!

"Yes," you say, "but how?"

Let's look again at those three areas of deception—in government, in homes, and in spiritual beliefs—to sum up the situation and find some answers.

Deception in Government

The Constitution pledges "life, liberty and the pursuit of happiness" yet the Supreme Court defends Roe v. Wade. The president of the United States promotes D & X abortion procedures, known as partial birth abortions, where all but the head a child has exited the mother's body.

The doctor inserts scissors at the base of the skull and literally sucks the brains of the child out with a syringe. The skull collapses and the child dies instantly.

The Clinton Administration says that the D & X procedure is "rare." The subservient liberal media parrots the word *rare* and the American people are deceived. How rare is it?

Recently a defender of this dreadful practice said flat out that it happens in only 1 percent of all abortions.[4] That means it happens 15,000 times a year or forty times every day. That's like a major plane crash, like the recent Valu-Jet or TWA crashes, every three-to-five days.

What's your definition of a really rare event? If a Valu-Jet went down every three days with 120 people on board each time, would you call it rare? Do you think the Federal Aviation Administration would be concerned? Remember, I am using the statistics of the defenders of the practice. It's really a lot worse. America has been deceived!

Abortions are dangerous. Most assume that a visit to an abortion clinic is a routine medical procedure. Wrong! Some women come out of abortion clinics sterile, with a perforated uterus and a permanent colostomy. Some die!

The question for Christians is What can we do about this?

We have petitioned Congress to no avail. We have stood beside the streets across the nation in quiet protest, holding posters saying, "Abortion Kills Babies" to no avail. The slaughter of the unborn continues.

Politicians live to get reelected. They get reelected with money, and Planned Parenthood gives millions to liberal politicians for radio, TV, and newspaper ads guaranteeing political victory. The evening television news with you standing in silent protest may get your congressman's ear—but not his vote.

I have a solution that will bring the abortion industry to a screeching halt. It cuts to the chase and gets to the bottom line instantly. It stops the flow of money into the abortion mills. Here's the plan.

We are constantly looking for any woman who has been medically injured in an abortion clinic: someone who has been rendered sterile, or come out with a punctured uterus, wearing a permanent colostomy.

When you find a woman who is willing and emotionally capable of enduring a lawsuit, file one against every doctor, nurse, and property owner of that abortion clinic.

Here is how it financially guts the abortion industry. First, each person sued has to find an attorney that will be paid by Planned Parenthood. Every dollar you force Planned Parenthood or any other pro-abortion agency to spend paying an attorney is one dollar less they will have to use in the slaughter of the unborn. One attorney on our side can cause many expensive attorneys to be necessary for the pro-abortion side.

Secondly, the defense of any personal injury case in an

abortion clinic can easily cost $100,000. Hit them in the wallet!

Thirdly, if you win the case, and with the right plaintiff, the advantage is yours, you can win a personal injury settlement in the millions of dollars. Remember, it took only one case in court to prove R.J. Reynolds Tobacco Company was liable for the cancer of cigarette smokers, which turned that whole industry upside down.

When aggressive Christians begin to file lawsuits by the dozens across America against abortion clinics, the insurance companies will see the danger of this exposure and dramatically raise insurance rates, which will drive many abortion clinics out of business.

Fourthly, there is the fear factor. Right now doctors and nurses in abortion clinics use their medical skills to crush the skulls of America's unborn babies and pull their mutilated bodies out in shreds with absolutely no fear of any consequence.

If the righteous will be "as bold as a lion" and cause these doctors, nurses, and property owners to be sued in the courts from coast to coast, the fear of financial ruin will force them to cease and desist.

Then there's deception in public education.

Deception in Public Education

Parents of America believe their children go to school to be educated in the disciplines of reading, writing, and arithmetic. Not so! Other countries are teaching their children this core curriculum; in America our children are being taught how to get in touch with their inner selves and to become subservient pawns of a global society.

As I mentioned in Chapter 4, the NEA has a special "National Charter," granted by Congress, allowing exemption from $1.6 million in real estate taxes on two Washington, D.C., office buildings with an estimated value of $65 million. I repeat, the NEA is a union with a political agenda.

Petition your congressman to strip the NEA of its "National Charter" and force it to pay taxes and to curb its lobbying activities and political campaigning. Get involved in your child's academic life. Go to PTA and school board meetings. Demand to know what your child is being taught. God gave you your children, they do not belong to the state or to the NEA. Do not live like a second class citizen begging for crumbs. Get informed and demand to be heard!

Another important educational issue is prayer in schools. Every believer in America must realize they have a constitutional right to pray in public schools *right now*! It's not necessary for Congress to pass any additional legislation.

I tell the children of my congregation, "If you want to pray in school, do it! If you want to pray over a test, before you get on the bus, at the flagpole, or over your meal, don't let anyone stop you. If a teacher or principal tries to stop you, call the church. We will file a lawsuit that day against that principal, that teacher, and that school district."

You may be thinking, *That's okay for you, pastor, your church is a megachurch. Our church doesn't have that kind of money.*

Maybe not. Still that needn't stop you. Two excellent organizations—The American Center for Law and Justice and The Rutherford Institute[5]—are willing to aid Christians who have justifiable grievances. We are not alone in this battle.

Always remember, those who do not use their freedoms to defend their freedoms will lose their freedoms.

What can we do about all this deception in government?

Here are seven steps you can take to expose deception in government:

1. Get informed and stay informed! Read your Bible and your newspaper and decide to take action.

2. Stop voting for liberal politicians whose "tax and spend" philosophy has America on the verge of bankruptcy. Stop listening to what politicians say and watch how they vote. Stop being deceived by symbolism over substance. Go into the voting booth and send righteous men and women to represent you locally, in your state, and in Washington, D.C.

3. Write and call your congressman and protest laws that infringe on your freedom to worship and teach your children godly principles.

4. Write and call your congressman and demand impeachment proceedings against federal judges who have hijacked the American Constitution and taken power from the people to impose their own godless, anti-religious agenda. It's time to advance the idea that the judge who violates the Constitution and violates the will of the people has committed a crime as great as that of any bank robber or rapist.

5. Call in and speak out on talk radio shows. Write letters to the editor when a newspaper editorial or column violates Christian beliefs.

6. After tithing to your church, give offerings to ministries that are speaking out "against principalities, against powers, against the rulers of the darkness"[6]—minstries that are taking the lead in fighting for your religious freedom.

7. Consider running for a local position—on your school board or local government—yourself. Or back a friend who will represent your values.

These are all legal, peaceful steps, which we can take to protect our rights. We are in no way disobeying those in authority in this country.

"Okay, pastor, I agree with these steps," you say. "But sometimes things still don't change. Is it ever right to disobey the government with God's blessing?"

Yes—but always peacefully. There is no room for violence.

Three Bible illustrations support *peaceful opposition.*

When Pharaoh commanded Egyptian midwives to drown male Jewish children, born to the Israelites, they refused to obey his order and God blessed them for their action.

Pharaoh was the civil authority. What he commanded, God condemned. The midwives disobeyed the Egyptian government with God's blessings.[7]

The second illustration is that of the wise men who went to worship Jesus Christ in Bethlehem's manger. They called on Herod and asked where the infant king was born.

Herod, a murderous paranoid monster, told them, "When you have found Him, bring back word to me, that I may come and worship Him also." The Bible says the wise men "departed for their country another way."[8]

Herod was the civil authority. He commanded the wise men to tell him where he might find Jesus. Divinely informed that Herod would kill the infant, they disobeyed the order of civil authority with heaven's blessing.[9]

The third illustration is found in the Book of Acts where the apostles were commanded to stop preaching in the name of Christ. They instantly disobeyed civil authority because the government commanded what God condemned.[10]

How does this apply to our society? When the president of the United States gives his support for homosexuals in the military, we stand with the Word of God—not the president.

When the government demands that our children go to public schools where they learn about putting condoms on bananas, life boat ethics, and the Rainbow Curriculum, which shows nine year olds how to have anal intercourse, it's time to remind the government that these children belong to us—not them. It's time to force the government to return the public schools to local control.

We can defeat deception in government. We can also defeat deception in our own marriages.

Deception in Marriage

Getting married is easy. Staying married is tough. A boob-tube generation of Americans has been brainwashed by Hollywood's version of the successful marriage. It appears effortless, and if asked to sacrifice, the instant answer is divorce. This is deception!

Marriage is a covenant. In the Bible, a covenant demands that the will of two people die and a sovereign unified will is born. Every marriage conflict comes because one or both in the marriage relationship refuses the crucified life. One or both wants their will at all costs. It becomes a rights fight.

We send our children to universities where they study for years to become teachers, doctors, and lawyers. Yet we allow them to leap into marriage, a relationship that creates life, that determines their happiness and well being, with little or no instruction in how to be a successful wife or husband.

We Are Deceived about Sex in Marriage

Paul's first command to men was "Let each man have his own wife."[11] Sex outside of marriage is absolutely forbidden. There are no excuses. God has zero tolerance. Safe sex is sex with a marriage license.

Paul's second command to man was "Let the husband render to his wife the affection due her."[12] He was referring to sex. Sex is not just for procreation. It's the symphony of the soul for married couples. It's joy. It's giving and sharing. It's tender and holy.

"The affection due her" means the payment of what is due. When you rent a house, the rent is payment of what is due. When you buy a car, the car note is payment of what is due. When you get married, sex is payment of what is due.

Men and women are deceived in marriage about what each other desires. Here are seven steps you can take to combat deception in your marriage:

1. Husbands, love your wives completely, passionately, and romantically. The Bible says, "Husbands love your wives just as Christ also loved the church and gave Himself for her."[13] In short, your wife wants a lover.

2. Remain faithful to each other. Women do not want a playboy husband. Playboy husbands will sooner or later come home with AIDS. Men don't want unfaithfulness either. God does not demand that any woman or man stay in a relationship that is repeatedly unfaithful.

3. Husbands, give your wives non-sexual affection. In counseling sessions, I have asked men and women this question. "How would you feel if you knew you could never have sex again with your mate?" Almost all women said, "It's really no big deal if I never have sex again with my husband. But it would be a big deal if we never touched or kissed or romanced again." That's non-sexual affection. Now when I ask men the same question, their eyes bulge, nostrils flare, and sweat pops out on their forehead. "Give up sex? Not in this life-time!" To ask a man to give up sex is like asking him to give up breathing.

4. Diana and I have something we call O.W.E. It means one way every day. Every day both of us do something to remind the other of our love and fidelity one for the other. Try it, you'll like it.

5. If you are both believers, read the Bible together. Do it early in the day.

6. Pray together. The Bible says, "A threefold cord is not quickly broken."[14] A man and his wife, bound together with God in prayer, is an unbreakable union.

7. Pray for each other. It's hard to treat someone unfairly if you are praying for them.

We can overcome deception in marriage. And we can overcome deception in spiritual beliefs.

Deception in Spiritual Beliefs

I mentioned four major areas of spiritual deception in America in Chapters 10 and 11: satanism, the goddess movement, clergy homosexuality, and errant philosophy and unusual manifestations of the spirit.

Let me add two others here briefly: denominationalism and racism.

Denominationalism is to approve of a person because he belongs to your brand of church. Denominationalism is idolatry. It's love for who you are, not what you are.

When I hold crusades in the metropolitan areas of America, denominationalism is ever present. If you invite the Baptists, the Pentecostals don't want to come, fearing it will be too formal. If you invite the Pentecostals, the Baptists don't want to come, fearing it will be too emotional. If you invite the Catholics, both Baptists and Pentecostals start quoting Scripture from Revelation 17.

The devil's crowd can come together in absolute unity over anything. God's crowd looks for a reason to reject anything spiritual not born by our respective denominations. The concept seems to be, "If we didn't think of it, neither has God!"

It's time to remove denominational barriers. As long as we agree on the inerrancy of the Word and blood atonement of the Cross, we should stand together in love.

A second area of spiritual deception is racism. Racism is very real in the church. Yet when you read the Word of God there is no white church, black church, brown church, red church, or yellow church. There is only the blood-bought church of Jesus Christ.

Too many churches are looking for members with the "right stuff." We need to open our doors to "whosoever will" with love and compassion. We are saving souls, not skins.

A black man tried to join a very proper all-white church in the deep South. His application for church membership was turned down six times. He stopped applying. After several months, he bumped into the pastor at the local supermarket. The pastor asked him, "Why did you stop applying for church membership?"

The black man responded, "It hurt my feelings at first, but I prayed about it and God said, 'Don't worry about it, I've been trying to get in that church for fifty years and they won't let me in either.'"

Racial barriers must also come down. All Christians are brothers and sisters of the King.

If I could summarize the doctrinal deception within the church in one sentence, it would be this: We have lost the centrality of the Cross of Jesus Christ in our preaching and teaching.

The apostle Paul wrote, "But God forbid that I should boast except in the cross of our Lord Jesus Christ."[15] The church has permission to boast in one thing: the Cross. Not stained glass windows. Not buildings. Not budgets and baptisms. Not pipe organs and prestigious memberships. Just the Cross.

What is the difference between the atheist who hates the church and the church member who says, "I love the church" but won't go to church. There is no difference. The end result is the same, neither goes to church.

What is the difference between the atheist who disbelieves the Bible and the man who says, "I believe the Bible," but he doesn't read the Bible? There is no difference.

The point is this: It isn't what you know, it's how you apply what you know. You can intellectually know the Sermon on the Mount. You can applaud it, but without the Cross you can never apply it.

The Cross is the source, the origin, and the center of every blessing. I am saved through the blood of the Cross of Christ. I am healed by the stripes on His back. The Cross guarantees a peace that surpasses understanding. Without the Cross even the act of prayer is an absolute waste of time.

Without the Cross we have ritual without righteousness, ceremony without change and hype without holiness.

How do you see the Cross?

Most go to the Cross for forgiveness of sin, but we refuse to go to the Cross and accept the crucified life. We do not want to die to self. We do not want to surrender our will for His will. We are willing for Christ to forgive our sins but don't crucify our flesh.

Do you see the suffering Son of God on the Cross? Who put Him there? God the Father! Why? Because His Son took upon Himself the sin of the world and it pleased God to pour out His wrath upon His own Son.

If it pleased God to pour out His wrath on His own Son because of sin, do you think for one instant God will excuse the sin in your life?

God could care less about your religious activity and your social standing. He is only interested in your relationship to His Son through the Cross. If there is no relationship, He will judge the sin in your life just as He did His own Son. The angels of God will escort you into the fires of an eternal hell.

If praise can puff you up, you are not dead to the flesh. If criticism can hurt you, you are not dead to the flesh. If persecution can stop you, you are not dead to the flesh.

Here are four action points for combating spiritual deception in the church:

1. Read the Bible every day. Underline passages that you fear are neglected or violated in your life.
2. If your church does not teach biblical truth, make an appointment with your pastor and share with him the verses you have read. If he and the elders don't listen, leave that church. Your commitment is to God, not that

church. The apostle Paul commands, "From such turn away."

3. Pay your tithes and offerings. This is obedience to God's Word. If good teaching is supported, it will prosper and grow. If it is not, it will wither and die.

4. If you are a member of a denomination where biblical values are being questioned, voice your opinions at national conventions. If you are not heard, then you must leave that denomination.

We must have an American reformation. Every Bible-believing Christian must make an absolute commitment to live by the standards of righteousness as prescribed in the Word of God.

There must be a new and fresh commitment to personal evangelism that burns like fire in our bones. America cannot be changed from the top down. Giving our money to elect a presidential candidate has proven an absolute fiasco. As soon as they win the nomination, they ignore the moral and spiritual values Christians cherish.

We can take America back one heart at a time, one home at a time, one church at a time, with a grassroots spiritual revolution created by winning the lost to Christ.

When a person gets saved, they become a member of an alternative society whose constitution and bylaws are written in the Word of God. We are not citizens of America. We are citizens of the kingdom of God.

As citizens of the kingdom, we do not condone in our government what God condemns. When the government condones what God condemns, our loyalty is with the Word of God.

Action is one of the weapons God has given us. He expects us to be obedient. "Doers of the word, and not hearers only."[16] But without faith, all of our works will amount to nothing. With faith, He can use even the little bit we give Him.

Faith Is the Key

With faith Jesus fed five thousand with a handful of loaves and fishes. With faith God kept a prophet, an old woman and her son alive for months with a handful of oil. It doesn't take much if God is in it. Your letter to the congressman isn't much but if you will pray, anoint it, and send it with faith, God will multiply its power and use it.

When Gideon told the angel that he was "the least," that God had obviously made a mistake, that he, Gideon, wasn't qualified, the angel answered back, "But God will be with you."

That's the difference. Out of the holocaust God gave birth to the modern state of Israel. Out of the darkness of an iron curtain, He is bringing revival and healing to many thousands whom no one ever thought had a chance.

"Let no man deceive you." Don't let it happen. Believe. Have faith.

Sunshine through the Fog

Finally there is one, last weapon God has given us to defeat the enemy. It is a spiritual weapon that can only be appreciated by those who have felt its power in time of crisis. When there is darkness, confusion, defeat, and deception, the Bible teaches God's people to praise Him, literally to rejoice.

Jesus said, "Blessed are you when men shall revile you and persecute you and say all manner of evil against you for my sake. Rejoice and be exceedingly glad. For great is your reward in heaven. For so persecuted they the prophets which were before you."[17]

The Israelites once experienced a time of great deception, parallel to what America is experiencing today. Their government became corrupted. Their youth intermarried with other tribes and violated all of God's many tender and merciful instructions for having a happy home. Their worship turned into idolatry and satanism.

Then someone rediscovered God's Word and began to read it. Soon the whole nation began to publicly read what the prophets had written. Great fear swept the nation as they realized their deception and the extent of their sin against God.

"What can we do?" they asked. "Should we divorce our heathen wives and find new ones? What a mess we are in."

The prophet Nehemiah stood up and called for attention. "This is no time for despair," he said. "This is a time to rejoice. We are rediscovering God's Word. We can't solve everything in one day. But we have begun the journey out of deception. Go home, prepare a feast. No one should work. It is a holiday. And *may the joy of the LORD be your strength!*"[18]

I don't know your situation. I don't know what is happening in your marriage, what is happening to your children, or what is happening in your church. I don't know what will happen to America, whether she will once again find her way or whether she will soon slip into the abyss that has engulfed so many great civilizations and poisoned so many noble ideals.

But I do know my Redeemer. He said He would be with you to the end of the world. He said He would never forsake you. If you have found Him, if you have given your life to Him, you and your family can be saved from the destruction to come.

The Bible makes it very clear that warnings of the end times are meant to give God's people an advantage, an edge. "Therefore comfort one another with these words."[19] Do what you can, be obedient to His Word. He may yet spare our nation. But even if He does not, even if we as a people are engulfed by our own sins and destroyed by the spirit of our days of deception, rejoice in God, in His salvation, in His protection.

"Look up and lift your heads, because your redemption draws near."[20]

Notes

Chapter 1

1. 1 Kings 18:13.
2. 1 Kings 19:4.
3. Rush Limbaugh, *The Limbaugh Letter,* (New York: EFM, February 1996), 5.
4. Tom Squitieri, *USA Today,* 27 November 1996, A1.
5. Report of the 1994 Senate Hearings.
6. This information came to me from a former senior White House staffer who had studied this issue for five years. According to the staffer, since 1986 the IRS has been recommending to the White House that all religious organizations lose their tax exempt status with the exception of churches and religious orders as defined by the IRS themselves. Billy Graham's evangelistic organization, for example, would be out of business. Curiously, only days after this conversation, a government agency called for the revocation of the tax exempt status of the Christian Coalition.
7. H.B. London, Jr., "The Pastor's Weekly Briefing," *Focus on the Family,* 4, no. 26, 28 June 1996.
8. Bob Woodward, *The Choice,* (New York: Simon and Schuster, 1996), 131.
9. "The Pastor's Weekly Briefing," 2.
10. "The Case Against Clinton," *Human Events,* 16 August 1996, 23.
11. Ibid. This quote was taken from a transcript of the telephone conversations between Gennifer Flowers and Bill Clinton as released to the *Star* in a New York press conference in January 1992.
12. Jack W. Germond and Jules Whitcover, *Mad as Hell: Revolt at the Ballot Box 1992* (New York: Warner Books, 1993), 420-421.
13. Taken from a personal interview with the White House aide.
14. "Stumbling into a Combat Zone," *Time,* 3 June 1996, 26.
15. Center for America Values, Box 91180, Washington D.C., 20090-1180, *The Clinton Record.*
16. Matt. 10:27.
17. See Matt. 14.
18. Luke 13:32.
19. Ps. 92:10.
20. Matt. 12:30.
21. James 4:4.
22. Anthony Read and David Fisher. *The Fall of Berlin* (New York: Da Capo Press, 1992), 7.
23. Ibid.
24. Gitta Sereny, *Albert Speer: His Battle With the Truth.* (London: MacMillan, 1995), 27.
25. Read and Fisher, 32.
26. Ibid, 294.
27. Eph. 5:6-13.
28. Cal Thomas, syndicated column, "Whitewater verdict reveals crime cover-up," *The Conservative Chronicles,* 3 June 1996.

29. Ibid.
30. Limbaugh, 4.
31. Thomas.
32. White House Press Conference, 22 April 1994.
33. Limbaugh, 5.
34. Ibid, 4.
35. Ibid, 5.
36. Ibid, 5.
37. Taken from an interview with a former White House staffer.
38. The House Government Reform and Oversight Committee issued their finding that President Clinton "engaged in an unprecedented misuse of the executive power, abuse of executive privilege and obstruction of numerous investigations into the travel office." The Committee said travel director Billy Ray Dale and his colleagues were dismissed so that Harry Thomason, a Hollywood producer friend of the Clintons, and Catherine Cornelius, a distant cousin of the President, could seek a share of the governments travel business. ("Clinton accused of leading wide travel-office cover-up" *Arizona Republic,* 19 September 1996. A3.)
39. Doug Bandow, *The Conservative Chronicle,* 26 June 1996, 4.
40. James B. Stewart, *Bloodsport* (New York: Simon Schuster, 1996), 260.
41. Limbaugh, 15.
42. Ibid, 5.
43. Ibid, 5.
44. Ibid, 5.
45. Ibid, 5.
46. Bandow, 5.
47. Limbaugh, 15.
48. Bandow, 4.
49. Jer. 3:9.
50. Ps. 12:8.
51. Rev. 22:15.

Chapter 2

1. Stewart, 260.
2. Ibid. (James Stewart, a journalist who was in contact with Hillary and originally encouraged by her to write a book, makes a rather remarkable statement in his book *Bloodsport.* Instead of sayng that no one can prove they were, in fact, having an affair, Stewart writes the opposite, saying that no one could prove that they weren't. Stewart adds that both Vince and Hillary's friends say they "weren't the type.")
3. Gary Aldrich, *Unlimited Access* (Washington: Regnery, 1996), 70.
4. "Innaccuracies Regarding Foster's Death," Microsoft Internet Explorer, 18 June 1996, 3.
5. "*60 Minutes'* Report on the Death of Vince Foster," House of Representatives, 26 October 1995 H11373.
6. Testimony of Mr. Burton, congressman from Indiana. House of Representatives, 26 October 1995, 3.

7. "Innaccuracies Regarding Foster's Death," Microsoft Internet Explorer, 18 June 1996, 1.
8. Chris Ruddy, *Pittsburg Tribune-Review*, 16 June 1995. (Gonzalez, interviewed long after the event, told a reporter that he thought the second wound was in the forehead. But after examining photos, Gonzalez told investiagtors for the independent counsel that trauma to the neck would be consistent with what he saw.)
9. "Innaccuracies Regarding Foster's Death," Microsoft Internet Explorer, 5.
10. "Innaccuracies Regarding Foster's Death," Microsoft Internet Explorer, 1.
11. Stewart, 260.
12. Aldrich, 77.
13. Testimony of Mr. Burton, congressman from Indiana, 4, and Microsoft Internet Explorer, 4.
14. Ibid.
15. Aldrich, 77.
16. "Witness Tampering," Microsoft Internet Explorer, 18 June 1996.
17. *New York Times,* as reported in the *Arizona Republic,* 28 August 1996, A6.
18. The obvious question was how had Foster gotten such a gun? Serial numbers showed that one part of the gun was purchased in Seattle, the other in Indianapolis. Was this a professional hit?
19. "*60 Minutes*' Report on the Death of Vince Foster," House of Representatives, 26 October 1995, H11373.
20. "Innaccuracies Regarding Foster's Death," Microsoft Internet Explorer, 3.
21. Testimony of Mr. Burton, congressman from Indiana.
22. According to one account, Foster had a Swiss bank account that "was emptied of $2.7 million a week before he died." Microsoft Internet Explorer, "Innaccuracies Regarding Foster's Death," 2.
23. *Esquire* magazine interview.
24. Ps. 10:2, 8, 12.

Chapter 3

1. Jerome Burn, editor, *Chronicles of the World* (London: Longman Group UK Ltd., 1989), 87.
2. Matt. 4.
3. Pat Robertson, *The New World Order* (Dallas: Word Publishers, 1991), 115.
4. Ibid, 35.
5. Peter Padfield, *Himmler* (New York: Henry Holt & Co., 1990), 148.
6. Francis Miller, *The Complete History of World War Two* (Chicago: Readers Service Bureau, 1945), 5.
7. John Barron, *Operation Solo* (Washington: Regnery, 1996), 54.
8. Robertson, 14.
9. Ibid, 7.
10. Robertson, 53-54.

11. Randall Baer, *Inside the New Age Nightmare* (Lafayette, La.: Huntington House, 1992), 13.
12. Ibid, 17.
13. London, "The Pastor's Weekly Briefing," 1-2.
14. Robertson, 112
15. I took this information from one of my sermons, and the exact source is on file at Cornerstone Church.
16. Willard Cantelon, *The Day the Dollar Dies* (Jacksonville, Fla.: Logos International, 1973).
17. Robertson, 124-130.
18. Ibid, 119.
19. Hag. 2:8.
20. Robertson, 53.
21. Ibid, 177.
22. I heard about this case at a legal seminar in Dallas/Fort Worth.
23. The exact source of this reference is on file at Cornerstone Church.
24. Gallup GO 84148, September 1992.
25. Matt. 10:22.
26. The exact source of this reference is on file at Cornerstone Church.
27. Robertson, 221.
28. The exact source of this reference is on file at Cornerstone Church.
29. John Feder, *Pagan America* (Lafayette, La.: Huntington House, 1993), 228.
30. Robertson, 90.
31. Ibid, 91.
32. Ibid, 95.
33. Dan. 7:7-8; 19-20.
34. Rev. 13:3.
35. Dan. 8:25, KJV.
36. The exact source of this reference is on file at Cornerstone Church.
37. Matt. 24:15-19.
38. Barron, 54.
39. Rev. 13:6, NIV.

Chapter 4

1. James J. Kilpatrick, syndicated column, 27 December 1995.
2. Christian Coalition Special Action Alert, 10 May 1996 (taken from the *Washington Times,* 27 April 1996), 1.
3. *Conservative Chronicle,* vol. 11, 10 January 1996, 4.
4. Gen. 1:26.
5. The exact source of this reference is on file at Cornerstone Church.
6. "Men Are Easy,' Judge says." *The Arizona Republic,* 16 August 1996, A13.
7. Isa. 40:23.
8. Prov. 22:28.
9. Rom. 13:1.
10. Dan. 2:20.
11. Prov. 21:1.
12. Ps. 75:6–7.

13. Dan. 5:4–6.
14. Ps. 107:2.
15. Prov. 28:4.
16. Jer. 33:3.
17. James 4:2.
18. Matt. 16:19.
19. Luke 10:19.
20. Ex. 19:6.

Chapter 5

1. Gen. 31:32.
2. Josh. 6:34.
3. John 4:22.
4. Prov. 17:13.
5. Ex. 20:12 and Eph. 6:2.
6. Deut. 27:20.
7. Zech. 5:3.
8. Ex. 20:4–5.
9. Matt. 12:30.
10. Larry Kahaner, *Cults That Kill* (New York: Warner Books, 1988).
11. Ps. 9:17.
12. The exact source of this reference is on file at Cornerstone Church.
13. The exact source of this reference is on file at Cornerstone Church.
14. Roger J. Vaughan and Edward W. Hill, ed. by Michael Barker, *Banking on the Brink* (Washington: Washington Post Co. Briefing Books, 1992).
15. Hos. 7:9.

Chapter 6

1. Feder, 21.
2. Matt. 12:4.
3. Gen. 1:22.
4. 1 Cor. 7:4.
5. Eph. 4:15.
6. See 1 Tim. 5:8.

Chapter 7

1. 1 Tim. 5:8, KJV.
2. 2 Thess. 3:10
3. *Conservative Chronicle,* vol. 11, 13 March 1996, 23.
4. Rush Limbaugh, *The Limbaugh Letter,* (New York: EFM, May 1993), 11.
5. Ex. 12:3.
6. Ex. 33:11.
7. Gen. 7:1.
8. Luke 16:19–31.
9. Ps. 119:11.
10. Luke 6:46 KJV.
11. Gen. 27:33.
12. Ps. 101:3.

13. Eph. 5:25.
14. Deut. 33:4–5.
15. Num. 14:11,12, KJV.
16. See Num. 14:13-19.
17. Deut. 11:21.
18. "Seven-Year Cold," *Life,* 1982.
19. Rom. 5:8.

Chapter 8
1. J. Hamilton, *Where Now Is Thy God?* (Grand Rapids, Mich.: Revell, 1969), 67.
2. John 1:11.
3. Luke 23:4, 14; John 18:38.
4. John 16:33.
5. Eph. 4:15.

Chapter 9
1. 2 Cor. 11:14.
2. See Matt. 25:32–46.
3. Johanna Michaelson, *Like Lambs to the Slaughter* (Eugene, Ore.: Harvest House Publishers), 267.
4. Matt. 25:41.
5. Kahaner, 218.
6. Isa. 14:13.
7. Matt. 7:15.
8. Gen. 3:1.
9. Luke 4.
10. *Los Angeles Times,* 19 October 1988, 21.
11. John 3:18.
12. 1 Peter 5:8.
13. Acts 2:21.
14. John 8:36.
15. Rev. 12:10.
16. Sereny.
17. Kahaner, back jacket of book.
18. Ibid, 183–185.
19. Bob Larson, *Satanism: The Seduction of America's Youth* (Nashville, Tenn.: Thomas Nelson Publishers, 1989), 29.
20. Ibid, 29.
21. Ibid, 30.
22. Ibid, 171.
23. Ibid, 109.
24. 1 Tim. 6:12.
25. Isa. 54:17.
26. John 10:10.
27. Matt. 12:30.
28. Matt. 28:18–20.
29. James 2:19.
30. James 4:7.

Chapter 10

1. John 8:44.
2. Matt. 24:4.
3. Thomas Oden, "Encountering the Goddess at Church." *Christianity Today,* 16 August 1993, 18.
4. Timothy Morgan, "Re-Imaging Labeled 'Reckless.'" *Christianity Today,* 18 July 1994, 49.
5. Susan Cyre, "Fallout Escalates Over 'Goddess' Sophia Worship." *Christianity Today,* 4 April 1994, 74.
6. James R. Edwards, "Earthquake in the Mainline." *Christianity Today,* 14 November 1994, 42.
7. "Re-Imagining God," Friday Plenary, Tape 2-2, Side A.
8. Ibid.
9. Edwards, 39.
10. Edwards, 43.
11. Edwards, 40.
12. Edwards, 43.
13. Edwards, 42.
14. Prov. 8:23.
15. Gen. 3:1.
16. Morgan, 49.
17. Rom. 1:22-27.
18. ENI, "US Methodists reaffirm ban on promoting homosexuality," *The Episcopal News Service,* 23 May 1996, 13-14.
19. James Solheim, "Preliminary hearing held in trial," *The Episcopal News Service,* 12 December 1995, 10.
20. The General Convention Edition of United Voice, 25 August 1994.
21. ENI, "US Methodists reaffirm ban on promoting homosexuality," 8.
22. James Solheim, "Seattle dean blesses relationship of gay couple." *The Episcopal News Service,* 23 May 1996, 15-16.
23. Ex. 4:24-26.
24. 2 Tim. 3:4-5.
25. "The Boys From Brazil," *Penthouse,* December 1996, 6.
26. Eph. 4:19.
27. Eph. 5:12.
28. *Penthouse,* 74.
29. ENI, "Homosexuality issue to dominate Presbyterian agenda," *The Episcopal News Service,* 25 June 1996, 41.
30. ENI, "US Methodists reaffirm ban on promoting homosexuality." 33.
31. Ex. 18:11.
32. Actually, the phenomena began in Lakeland, Florida, almost a year earlier. *Charisma* magazine chose to publicize the Toronto experience and so it was dubbed by their writers as the "Toronto Blessing." The name stuck.
33. Laurence J. Barber, "How I Was Blessed," *Christianity Today,* 11 September 1995, 26.
34. James A. Beverly, "Toronto's Mixed Blessing," *Christianity Today,* 11 September 1995, 24.

35. "Toronto Church Ousted From Vineyard," *Charisma,* February 1996, 12.
36. George Byron Koch, "Pumped and Scooped," *Christianity Today,* 11 September 1995, 25, adapted from the Spiritual Counterfeits Project Newsletter, Berkeley, California, Spring 1995.
37. Ibid.
38. Ibid.
39. Gal. 5:22.
40. 1 John 4:1.
41. 1 Thess. 5:21.
42. 1 John 2:15.

Chapter 11

1. James 2:19
2. James 2:20.
3. Judg. 6:14.
4. "The Pastor's Weekly Briefing," *Focus on the Family,* 4, no. 48, 29 November 1996, 2.
5. If you want to report a violation of your religious rights or are seeking information about legal issues pertaining to religion, you can write to the American Center for Law and Justice, P.O. Box 64429, Virginia Beach, VA 23467, (804) 579-2489 or the Rutherford Institute, P.O. Box 7482, Charlottesville, VA 22906, (804) 978-3888 to report an incident or (800) 441-3473 to request information from the institute's radio show, "Freedom Under Fire," about a particular legal issue. The Rutherford Institute can also be reached by e-mail—rutherford@fni.com—or check out their web site at http//www.rutherford.org.
6. Eph. 6:12.
7. See Ex. 2.
8. Matt. 2:8, 12.
9. Matt. 2:12.
10. Acts 4:18-31.
11. 1 Cor. 7:2.
12. 1 Cor. 7:3.
13. Eph. 5:25.
14. Eccl. 4:12.
15. Gal. 6:14.
16. James 1:23.
17. Matt. 5:10-12.
18. Neh. 8:9-10.
19. 1 Thess. 4:18.
20. Luke 21:28.

HAGEE'S NUMBER #1
Bestseller

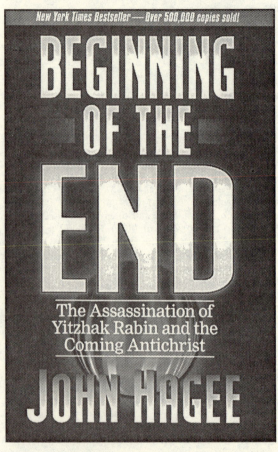

New York Times Bestseller — Over 500,000 copies sold!

BEGINNING OF THE END

The Assassination of Yitzhak Rabin and the Coming Antichrist

JOHN HAGEE

Beginning of the End
The Assassination of Yitzhak Rabin and the Coming Antichrist

Noted pastor John Hagee asks the tough questions about the 1995 assassination of the Israeli prime minister, and how it fits into the events prophesied centuries ago in the Bible.

0-7852-7370-0 • Trade Paperback • 208 pages